A Guide to

Everyday Economic Statistics

A Guide to

Everyday Economic Statistics

Seventh Edition

Gary E. Clayton

Martin Gerhard Giesbrecht

Feng Guo

 Higher Education

 Higher Education

Published by McGraw-Hill/Irwin, a business unit of The McGraw-Hill Companies, Inc., 1221 Avenue of the Americas, New York, NY, 10020. Copyright © 2010, 2004, 2001, 1998, 1995, 1992, 1990 by The McGraw-Hill Companies, Inc. All rights reserved. No part of this publication may be reproduced or distributed in any form or by any means, or stored in a database or retrieval system, without the prior written consent of The McGraw-Hill Companies, Inc., including, but not limited to, in any network or other electronic storage or transmission, or broadcast for distance learning.

Some ancillaries, including electronic and print components, may not be available to customers outside the United States.

♲ This book is printed on acid-free paper.

1 2 3 4 5 6 7 8 9 0 DOC/DOC 0 9

ISBN   978-0-07-352319-4
MHID   0-07-352319-4

Vice president and editor-in-chief: *Brent Gordon*
Publisher: *Douglas Reiner*
Director of development: *Ann Torbert*
Development editor: *Anne E. Hilbert*
Vice president and director of marketing: *Robin J. Zwettler*
Associate marketing manager: *Dean Karampelas*
Vice president of editing, design and production: *Sesha Bolisetty*
Lead project manager: *Pat Frederickson*
Lead production supervisor: *Michael R. McCormick*
Design coordinator: *Joanne Mennemeier*
Cover design: *Joanne Mennemeier*
Typeface: *Times New Roman*
Compositor: *S4Carlisle Publishing Services*
Printer: *R. R. Donnelley*

www.mhhe.com

About the Authors

Gary E. Clayton is Professor and Chair of the Economics & Finance Department at Northern Kentucky University. His Ph.D. in economics is from the University of Utah and he is the only American with an Honorary Doctorate from the People's Friendship University of Russia (PFUR) in Moscow. He has appeared on numerous radio and television programs and for two years was a regular guest commentator on economic statistics for NPR's *Marketplace*. In addition to his other writings and newspaper commentary, he has published five textbooks in the middle school, high school and college markets, including the best-selling *Economics: Principles and Practices* with Glencoe Publishing. Professor Clayton's web portal, www.EconSources.com, was described as "among the most useful [sites] on the web" by the Federal Reserve Bank of Boston's *Ledger*.

Dr. Clayton has taught international business and economics to students in London, Austria, and Australia. He is interested in the economic advancement of developing nations and in 2006 helped organize a micro loan project in Uganda. He is a year 2000 Freedoms Foundation Leavey Award winner for Excellence in Private Enterprise Education, an Association of Real Estate License Law Officials (ARELLO) national Consumer Education Award winner, and the recipient of a national teaching award from the National Council on Economic Education. In 2005 Dr. Clayton was the recipient of Northern Kentucky University's Frank Sinton Milburn Outstanding Professor Award.

.

Martin Gerhard Giesbrecht is Professor Emeritus of Economics at Northern Kentucky University. He has taught and/or conducted research at Stanford University, the University of Chicago, Harvard University, Indiana University, National Chengchi University (Taiwan), Rutgers University, and Wilmington College. His doctoral degree (cum laude) was earned at the University of Munich, Germany, which he attended on a Fulbright Grant. Making economics accessible, intellectually enlightening, and even entertaining is the mission of Martin Giesbrecht's professional life. All of his twelve books, including this one, and his many shorter articles, some of which have also appeared in German and Chinese, are dedicated to that end, as are his weekly radio commentaries on WNKU and WMKV.

Because he writes and speaks in a way that people can understand, the Society of Professional Journalism bestowed the Award for Excellence on him in 1993. He has also won awards from the German-American Chamber of Commerce, the National Aeronautics and Space Administration (NASA), the American Society for Engineering Education, the National Science Foundation, the General Electric Foundation, the Ford Foundation, the U.S. Small Business Administration, and the National Endowment for the Humanities, among others. He is especially gratified that the ΦΒΛ (Future Business Leaders) Fraternity voted him their favorite professor on the NKU campus.

Feng Guo is a Senior Research Economist at the Center for Economic Analysis and Development in Northern Kentucky University. Prior to taking up his present position, Dr. Guo was an economist with The Conference Board in New York City for four years. While at The Conference Board, Dr. Guo specialized in the development of business cycle indicators for China and in forecasting the aggregate economic activities for East Asian economies.

Dr. Guo's research has been published in several leading academic journals. His work has been widely cited and discussed by international agencies and central banks including the Australian Treasury, Bank of Japan and Hong Kong Monetary Authority, among others. Dr. Guo obtained his Ph.D. in Economics from the Graduate Center, City University of New York, his master's degree in Economics from Rissho University in Tokyo, Japan and his bachelor's degree in Business Administration from Shuren University in China.

Acknowledgements

For almost two decades now, through the many editions of this little book, we have benefited from the generous help, advice, comments, and suggestions of hundreds of economists, statisticians, journalists, financiers, students, leaders in industry and government, and other interested readers. We continue to be enormously grateful to them all. Beginning with this edition, we are proud to welcome Feng Guo, as a third co-author. And finally, we gratefully acknowledge Sherry Hulse for her careful checking and proofreading efforts. Any errors that remain, of course, are entirely our responsibility.

Table of Contents

Preface

Six years have passed since the last edition of this little guide was published. Unfortunately—or fortunately—the world and our economy are undergoing remarkable changes, and the future seems more uncertain than it has in a long time. In the absence of some kind of sophisticated GPS system in the sky that can show us all of the relevant statistical information that tells us where we are and how to get to where we want to go, almost every scrap of statistical economic information generated right here on the ground now becomes potentially very useful.

Yet, to some people, these economic statistics, like so many other numbers, seem as dry as an old bus schedule. The closer we look at them, however, the more they reveal themselves to be quite fascinating. There are two reasons for this. One, economic statistics hit us where we can feel them: in our breadbaskets, in our wallets, in our standards of living, and in our careers. And, two, they are themselves some of the more extraordinary and applicable achievements of our modern, technologically advanced age.

Everyday economic statistics do much more than keep track of events. They tell us where we have been and where we might be going. In doing so, they help us make important personal, family, and business decisions. To ignore them would be like flying blind or driving cross country without a GPS, or even a road map, which, to be sure, is possible but not advisable.

We can think of several more good reasons as to why we need to keep abreast of the tools, *our tools*—the economic statistics—that we use so often.

First, our statistics are constantly evolving. They are regularly updated. The samples on which some of them are based, such as the market basket of consumer goods and services from which the Consumer Price Index is calculated, are adjusted to reflect changing consumer buying behavior. The sets of statistical series included in various indices are similarly adjusted to our changing economic structure. And other technical, methodological, and definitional revisions are made to increase the accuracy of the economic picture they create.

Second, it is only natural that some statistics take on more importance—and others less so—as time goes on. The political responses to our recent economic difficulties have made government fiscal policies—government expenditures and taxes—more important than they have been for several decades. International investment and trade have also become bigger issues during that time. Without up-staging older, more familiar economic statistics, the data reporting on these newer concerns have moved closer to center stage.

Third, accessibility to our economic data continues to evolve. Twenty years ago, many of the individual series that economists used to keep track of the economy were available on the ECONOMIC BULLETIN BOARD at the U.S. Department of Commerce for a relatively modest cost. In 1995, and as part of a cost-saving measure, many of the most important business cycle series were transferred from the Bureau of Economic Analysis to The Conference Board, a private, non-profit business organization (where they were sold to users at a significantly higher cost). Since then, most federal data-generating agencies have put their data on the Internet, thereby increasing accessibility and lowering the cost to users. Most of the federal sites now have data extraction utilities that allow users to retrieve a staggering amount of data in a wide variety of formats. And, easy access to some of this wealth of available data is provided by www.EconSources.com.

Fourth, we continue to be overwhelmed and generally fascinated with numbers. Data are gathered continuously and released daily. Press releases from private and public statistical sources are picked up and quoted virtually verbatim by the media as if they were doctrine—and all the while we are left to sort it out.

And that's where this little book becomes especially important. It has no axe to grind. It is neither a statistics lecture nor an economics textbook. Instead, it is a handy little guide that can be consulted for clarification whenever any of the statistical series dealt with herein are encountered. It examines how different series are constructed and how we may use them effectively. Above all, it tries to put things in context, so the reader can see how an individual statistic relates to the larger picture. Because of this, you won't have to read the book consecutively from beginning to end, although that is OK, too.

In spite of troubles at home and around the world, many economies and the people living in them are doing better and have better prospects for the future than they have ever had. Countries around the world that were once mired in communism's dogmas or caught in the grip of poverty and underdevelopment are climbing out of these entrapments. And even with our own minor and major setbacks, America seems to have reached an entirely new level of economic performance that is still the envy of the rest of the world.

And let's be cautioned: in good times, it might seem less urgent to keep an eye on economic statistics. After all, we may put off watching our diets or keeping tabs on our blood pressures when we are in robust health. But, as more than a few of us have learned, this is also a time when concern about our personal well-being is critical. And the same goes for our economic well-being.

That is what this book is all about. Use it well, and use it often.

Gary E. Clayton
Martin Gerhard Giesbrecht
Feng Guo

Chapter 1

INTRODUCTION

How the Statistics in This Book Were Chosen

We need economic statistics to know how we are doing, and we need to know how we are doing in order to figure out how to get where we want to go. Decision making requires knowledge, and knowledge is the only logical basis of action. That is why we need economic statistics.

The problem is that there are literally millions of statistical series! At the personal level, each of us could probably generate a dozen series from our grocery receipts, odometer readings, telephone bills and electricity bills. Every business, town, city, county and industry could do, and often does, the same in its own field of operation.

Even the broad-based measures of economic statistics, those that deal with whole states, regions, and nations, number into the thousands. A glance at any statistical yearbook or almanac or at the annual *Statistical Abstract of the United States*[1] will make this point.

Yet, only a handful of economic statistical series are dealt with in this book. Why?

First and most obvious, there is such a thing as too much information. It can prevent us from seeing the forest for all the trees.

Second, many statistical series, like one detailing our own personal electricity consumption, are just not interesting to everyone.

---

[1] This publication is available from the Superintendent of Documents, U.S. Government Printing Office, Washington, D.C. 20402. The entire *Statistical Abstract* is also available on the web and can be accessed through the "U.S. Government Publications" section of the http://www.EconSources.com web site.

Third, many statistical series are compiled and published too late to be of much more than historical interest.

Finally, many statistical series are not reported regularly in the press and broadcast media, and are therefore of less interest.

However, other statistics have extremely high profiles. Some, like the Dow Jones Industrial Average, are reported daily on television, radio, in newspapers and on the Internet. Others, like the prime rate, are mentioned less frequently, but still receive prominent attention. Even others, like auto sales, are important because they tell us how a particular sector of the economy is performing.

If we want to know how we are doing or where we are headed, even a handful of series are usually more than enough. They include most of the major economic indicators that are important all of the time. Consumer confidence, the consumer price index, and the unemployment rate would certainly be in the top half-dozen of anyone's list of key economic statistics. Many others are important most of the time, and the rest are important at least some of the time.

We may not have selected everyone's favorite statistics for this little book—and for that we apologize—but we are driven by a positive philosophy of wanting to describe "what is" rather than a normative one of "what should be." The popular press may neglect some statistics when they should not be, while others are widely reported when there is less reason to do so. However, the objective here is to provide a guide to those series that *do* receive the attention rather than to the ones that *should*.

A Frame of Reference

The main measure of overall economic and business activity is gross domestic product (GDP), whose fluctuations are the most important gauge of good times or bad times that we have. Because GDP is defined as the total dollar value of all new final goods and services produced in a country during a one-year period, GDP is to be understood as a final, bottom-line accounting measure, an economic result, rather than as an indicator of things to come.

Many of the statistics reviewed in this book measure either the whole or parts of GDP. Other statistics, the index of leading indicators preeminent among them, serve better as signals of things to come. There are also more specialized series, such as the Standard & Poor's 500 (S&P 500), that serve both as general indicators of future economic activity and as first-order indicators for their own industries. Finally, we have other series such as new housing starts that provide important information for their own industries, but less value as indicators of future economic activity.

As we peruse the formal world of economic statistics, bear in mind that they cannot be evaluated in a vacuum. Statistical series need a background, or a frame of reference, so that they can be put in proper perspective. This the book attempts to do. Sometimes the frame of reference is discussed in terms of the historical development and evolution of the series. Or, the perspective may take the form of a detailed discussion of the way the statistic is measured and compiled. The frame of reference may also be the way the particular indicator or statistic relates to other developments in the economy. In the end, our goal is to provide a perspective that allows for proper interpretation and application of the particular series.

Of particular interest are the three types of indicators—leading, coincident, and lagging—shown in Figure 1-1. The name given to each refers to the way the series moves in relation to changes in overall economic activity. For example, the series marked "leading indicator" turns down before the economy enters a recession (indicated by the shaded area in the figure) and turns up before the expansion begins.

The "lagging indicator" series behaves just the opposite—it turns down after the economy enters a recession, and up after the recovery is underway. A coincident indicator neither leads nor lags. Instead, its timing is such that it turns down when the economy turns down, and up when the economy turns up.

Sometimes a series may lead a peak (the relative high) and/or a trough (the relative lows) in the economy and at other times it may lag a peak and/or trough. When this happens, the series is simply thought to be "unclassified" for forecasting purposes.

Whenever possible, the economic series examined in this book are plotted against the historical background of recessions and expansions in the manner illustrated in Figure 1-1. As will be seen, many series behave like those in the figure, although the timing of the

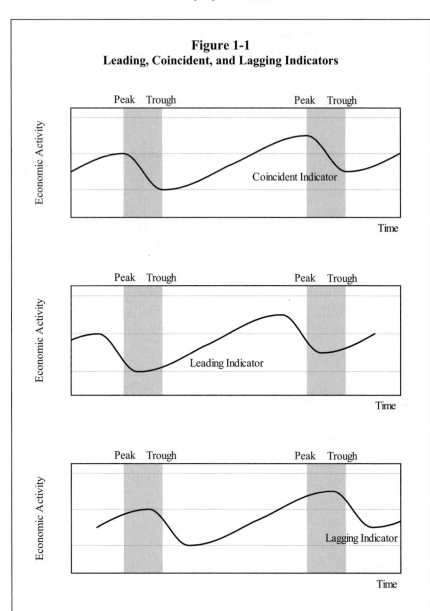

Figure 1-1
Leading, Coincident, and Lagging Indicators

Economists use the convention of shading recessionary periods to distinguish them from periods of expansion. Economic series are classified as leading, coincident, or lagging indicators depending on how their turning points—their peaks and troughs—compare to changes in the overall economy.

Leading indicators get most of the attention because they tend to go up or down before the economy goes up or down, and in so doing give us a warning as to where the economy may be headed.

turning points will vary considerably. Others will appear to have little, if any, relationship to changes in the overall economy. Even so, we feel that the presentation is important if you are to make your own judgments about the behavior of the series.

Finally, we also provide a brief summary of the statistical series that includes its status as an economic indicator, the source agency that compiles the data, the frequency of release, and other key information at the end of every section. In addition, current updates to most of these series, along with press releases, data retrieval tools, background articles, and even related web sites can be found in the *Everyday Economic Statistics* section of the www.EconSources.com web site.

The Many Faces of Economic Statistics

The task of interpreting economic statistics might seem to be a simple one: just take the numbers and describe how they changed from one period to the next. Unfortunately, it's not always that easy because most statistical series can be reported in a number of ways.

To illustrate, consider a hypothetical report stating that total sales increased by 5 percent from $800 billion to $840 billion over a recent 12-month period. If the report is in terms of current prices, and many initial reports are released this way, then it stands to reason that some of the $40 billion increase is due to inflation.

To compensate for inflation, sales can be measured in terms of "real," "constant," or "chain-linked" dollars using prices that prevailed in an earlier year.[2] If 2000 is used as the base year, and assuming that prices are approximately 10 percent higher now than they were in that base year, the same report could be worded like this: "In terms of chained (2000) prices, total sales increased from $720 billion to $738 billion for the most recent year." This time the increase of $18 billion is only a 2.5 percent gain, so half of the current dollar increase was due to inflation, the other half was due to real growth.

---

[2] In January of 1996, the U.S. Department of Commerce switched from a system of base-year fixed prices to a system using chain-weighted geometric averages with 1992 as the reference year. In 1999, the base year was updated to 1996 and it is now 2000. This technique is described more fully in the Appendix.

Most series that are susceptible to the distortions of inflation are reported in both current (nominal) and real (constant 2000 or chained 2000) dollar amounts. Both kinds of information are valuable—if used correctly—although the availability of both means that sales statistics can be reported in a number of different and seemingly confusing ways: [3]

- the final *current* or *nominal* dollar value of total sales ($840 billion)
- the change in the *current* or *nominal* dollar value of total sales ($40 billion)
- the final *chained, constant,* or *real* dollar value of total sales ($738 billion in 2000 dollars)
- the change in *chained, constant,* or *real* dollar value of total sales ($18 billion in 2000 dollars)
- the percentage change in the *current* or *nominal* dollar sales (5.0 percent, or $40 billion/$800 billion)
- the percentage change in *chain-weighted, constant,* or *real dollar sales* (2.5 percent, or $18 billion/$720 billion in 2000 dollars)

We have a similar problem when numbers are converted to an index, such as the consumer price index, the producer price index, or any other index. For example, suppose that the index under consideration has a base year of 1977 = 100 and currently stands at 145. If the index goes to 146 in the next month, there is an increase of 1 over the base period activity, or a 0.69 percent increase in the index over the previous month (1/145 = 0.0069). If the index were to grow at the same rate for each of the next 11 months, the annualized rate would be 8.6 percent. [4]

---

[3] Unfortunately the terms that economists use to describe numbers that are—or are not—distorted by inflation can be an endless source of confusion. While we tend to use some terms interchangeably in the text, the following guide may be of help when it comes to sorting out the differences. Specifically:

- Series adjusted for inflation are described as being in *constant dollar, real dollar,* or *chained* (where chaining is the inflation adjustment technique used) *dollar* amounts.
- Series *not* adjusted for inflation are described as being in *current* or *nominal* dollar amounts. If nothing is said about the series, as in "GDP this year is expected to be $11 trillion," then *current* (unadjusted) numbers are assumed.

[4] The series is compounding monthly, and so the correct computation is as follows:

$$\text{Annualized growth} = (1 + \text{monthly percentage change})^{12} - 1$$
$$= (1 + 0.0069)^{12} - 1 = 0.086$$

Because of compounding, you cannot multiply the monthly percentage change of 0.0069 by 12 to get an annualized rate, although this mistake is often made!

Using the numbers in the paragraph above, we can see that the change in any index can be reported in several different ways:

- the *absolute level* of the index (145)
- the *absolute change* in the level of the index from period to period (1)
- the *relative percentage change* from the previous period (0.69 percent)
- an *annualized projection* of the current period percentage change (8.6 percent)

In general, the relative percentage change is the most useful, with the annualized version coming in next. However, the reader should be advised that even these lists are not exclusive. For example, sometimes the change in the level of the index is compared to a period 12 months earlier. If the new level of 146 is 10 points higher than it was 12 months ago, then we could also say that the annual increase was closer to 7.35 percent.

Abusing Economic Statistics

The governments of most modern, industrialized nations of the free world—the United States among the best of them—enjoy a remarkable reputation for producing honest statistics. Many of these same countries also have a number of nongovernmental agencies that produce high-quality statistical series as part of a public service effort to gain acclaim and acceptance for their organizations. In some nations however, statistics are exaggerated, underreported, or simply faked for political or ideological reasons. When this happens, the usefulness of the statistics is radically reduced. Whether they know it or not, it is also a tragic loss to those nations that support this type of activity.

In the United States, our statistics tend to be brutally honest. Agencies that report their statistics normally publish release schedules months in advance of the actual release, and the methodology used to compile the series is remarkably open. As a result, there is not even the slightest hint that the release of new statistical figures is delayed in order to prevent some political or commercial embarrassment.

Abuse, however, does occur.

Perhaps the most common abuse of economic statistics is to apply them to situations for which they were never intended. For example, some series with little, if any, relationship to movements of the overall economy are often treated as if they are significant predictors of future changes in GDP. Personal income in current dollars, discussed in detail in Chapter 2, is one such example. The historical record shows that personal income almost always goes up, even when the economy is in recession.[5] Even so, increases in personal income are dutifully reported and widely heralded by the press each time they are released.

Other series are treated as indicators of future economic activity when, in fact, they are actually coincident or lagging indicators. Interest rates can be cited in this context, especially the prime rate which consistently lags changes in real GDP. Changing interest rates certainly affect selected sectors of the economy, especially housing, automobiles, and to some extent stock prices, but changing interest rates are of little use in predicting future changes in the direction of the overall economy.

Yet another abuse is to focus on nominal dollar values when the real, or inflation-adjusted, figures give a better picture of the underlying changes. Unfortunately, various government agencies sometimes contribute to this problem because the nominal dollar data and the price deflators needed to adjust the data are not available at the same time. When the U.S. Department of Commerce releases its *Advance Monthly Retail Sales* report during the second week of every month, the data are adjusted for seasonal, holiday, and trading day differences, but not for inflation. By the time inflation-adjusted figures are finally available, the initial change in retail sales has already been reported and the new figures are of little interest to the media.

Finally, we should note that the media sometimes report on new economic figures without giving us enough information to evaluate the significance of the numbers. It is not at all unusual to hear that a particular index has gone up, say, 4 points, without any mention of the overall level of the index. Four points on a basis of 40 is one thing, but 4 points on an index with a value of 400 may be quite another. In fact, changes in the Dow Jones Industrial Average are often reported this way, as in "the market was up today, increasing a total of 60 points."

---

[5] See the discussion of personal income on pages 33 through 35.

Using Economic Statistics

Some decision making may require an understanding of other economic conditions, perhaps those that occur at a regional or industry level. Even if the data you need are not described in these chapters (as most of the statistics in this book pertain to the national economy), you should be able to use the methods described here to build your own set of economic indicators.

If you do, remember that every statistical series has its own distinct personality. If you want to use a series, examine it carefully and try to see how it relates to your own situation. For example, are series measured in real, rather than nominal, dollars better for your application? Also, you might examine the series to see if changes in the series are more important than the absolute level of the series.

And, what about the timing of the series? If it lags, then it may not be of much help. If it leads, then you may have to spend more time trying to anticipate its movements. If you need regional or industry-specific data, don't forget to look for other sources of data generated by state departments of economic development, chambers of commerce, economic development districts, local universities, and industry and trade publications.

One practical way of organizing economic statistics for your own use is to build your own historical database of the statistical series that are especially important to you. You can do this with an appropriate spreadsheet program on your personal computer and then chart or otherwise present the results. Yearly entries are probably sufficient for the bygone years, but quarterly and monthly data for more recent times will keep you more up-to-date.

To monitor overall economic conditions, you may want to keep tabs on GDP, the consumer price index, the unemployment rate, and several other series, such as the index of leading indicators. To zero in on your own individual area of concern, focus on those series that affect this area more directly. For example, you would examine consumer spending and retail sales if your concern is retail marketing, or the Dow Jones Industrial Average and Standard & Poor's 500 if you are more concerned with the stock market.

As your sophistication grows, this accumulation of statistical data will not only reveal the current state of affairs to you, but you will also begin to be able to discern the development of trends. Being able to do this on your own, rather than relying on the news media, gives you that decisive competitive edge that is so important in today's business world. It's mighty useful in your personal affairs too.

Don't be afraid to be creative. If the statistics enable you to perceive your economic reality, your economic reality may also enable you to anticipate the statistics. This can be very useful. For example, if your decision is to refinance a mortgage, and if you are waiting for the lowest possible rates, it helps to know that interest rates usually go down during a recession and continue to go down well into the subsequent recovery.

So, if the economy appears to be just entering a recession, it might be wise to postpone the refinancing for another year or so. Or, if the expansion is well underway, you may want to refinance immediately since interest rates have a history of increasing late in the recovery. In either case, knowledge of how a series relates to the overall economy can be helpful in a number of ways.

Finally, bear in mind that—until you become more familiar with the statistics in this book—you don't even have to be an expert to know if the economy is in a recession or an expansion. Just stay tuned to the news, and the media will keep you abreast of developments. Of course the media may miss the beginning or ending of a recession by six months or so—but be especially suspect of politicians who make proclamations about the state of the economy during an election year as they may be trying to distort the real situation for personal political gain. For the most part, however, those who report on national economic developments in the media usually do a reasonably good job of keeping us posted on the state of the economy.

And Beware of Forecasts!

With all of this said, we should also point out that none of this is a formal theory nor a method for making forecasts. Much longer books than this have dealt unsuccessfully with that subject. But we do encounter many large and small forecasts in our daily lives, and these contain fertile opportunities for making statistical trouble.   Be forewarned! Here are some things to look out for:

Point Forecasts   These are the most common, but they are often wrong because outcomes are unlikely to reach the predicted point precisely. For example, if we predict that the GDP next year will be $15 trillion, we have an almost 100 percent chance of being wrong because next year's GDP might turn up to $15 trillion and 1 cent or any other such number.

Interval Forecasts   It is better to say that next year's GDP will be $15 trillion, give or take $50 billion. That means the forecast will turn out to be correct if next year's GDP falls between $14.95 and $15.05 trillion.

Probability Forecasts   It is even better to say that next year's GDP has an 85 percent probability of being between $14.95 trillion and $15.05 trillion. This way the confidence with which the forecast is made can be expressed. The higher the probability, the more believable the forecast will appear to be, assuming that the forecaster is reputable.

Unconditional Forecasts   All of the above examples fall into this category because, unlike the conditional forecast below, they are not premised on some second event taking place.

Conditional Forecasts   "There is an 85 percent probability that next year's GDP will be between $14.95 trillion and $15.05 trillion if the Federal Reserve System does not raise the discount rate" is a conditional forecast because all bets are off if the Fed does raise the discount rate. This gives the forecaster an "out" if the forecast turns out to be wrong, but it also makes the forecast a bit less useful to the user.

Event Forecasts   All the above examples fall into this category, because they deal with a single event, a single outcome.

Time Series Forecasts   A series of forecasts that march into the future by convenient time steps—months, quarters, or years—are much more complicated than a single-event forecast. For example, forecasting that "the GDP next year will grow at an annual rate of 4 percent during the first 6 months and then slow to 3 percent in the last half of the year" is actually making at least two forecasts. Since the second one is probably dependent on the accurate outcome of the first, this kind of forecasting can be tricky. Rate-of-change over time forecasts are especially susceptible to this complication.

Extrapolation Forecasts   Extrapolation from a monthly figure is often taken as a kind of time series forecast. For example, a monthly increase of 0.69 percent converts to an annual rate of 8.6 percent, if the next 11 months are identical to the most recent one (see footnote 4 for the computation).

Weighted Moving Average Forecasts   If a particular series is subject to considerable fluctuation, a moving average with specific weights assigned to earlier periods can be used to smooth the data. When this technique is adapted to forecasting, it is easier to predict the next number in the average since a portion of the data used to construct it is already in hand. And, with our attention focused on the moving average, the forecaster can even be excused if the next new observation "deviates" from the mean.[6]

Many of the forecasts that we encounter in the daily news have considerable value. Many others, however, have little or no value since we are not clear as to what kind of forecast they are or how they have been constructed. They often use hedging or waffling language that, when carefully examined, pulls the rug of credibility out from underneath them. Even worse, many are based on other statistics that may not be well suited for the forecast being made.

A Final Word

Throughout, this book tries to be ideologically and theoretically neutral, or at least conventional. Notice that the economic indicators described in the following chapters are grouped primarily by economic function rather than by alphabet or other method. This is to recognize implicitly that, while no formal theoretical or ideological statement is intended, our economy is nevertheless a functioning system made up of identifiable parts that somehow work together.

And remember: we should never become so blinded by the apparent numerical precision and by the "scientific," "theoretical," or "official" nature of these economic indicators that we ignore our own sensitivity to economic and business conditions. Our own observations may be rather parochial, but they are immediate and undisputably real. Keeping an eye on the amount of construction activity in the neighborhood where we live, the type of cars that we and our neighbors drive, the intensity of traffic on our streets, how hard or easy it is to find a place to park, what and how much people are buying in the stores where we shop, the number of layoffs or job promotions among our friends and acquaintances, the level of maintenance and upkeep in our surrounding buildings and grounds,

---

[6] Statistics on changes in manufacturing and trade inventories are smoothed using a four-term weighted average with weights of 1, 2, 2, and 1. To illustrate, changes of $-47.2, $68.2, $64.1, and $40.3 billion (the numbers for June, July, August, and September of a given year) yield a moving average of $42.95 billion for the month of September.

and even the changes in the frequency of marriages and new babies in our communities can all be very revealing. We ourselves are, after all, living daily in the very economy we are trying to understand.

This economic awareness, this "feel" for business conditions, should be extended to our interpretations of the statistical series as well. We can examine the way statistical series are constructed, and we can look at the historical record to see how they behave. But in the end, it comes down to developing a feel for what they really tell us.

Chapter 2

TOTAL OUTPUT and INCOME

Gross Domestic Product

The most comprehensive measure of production is **gross domestic product (GDP)**–the market value of all final goods, services, and structures produced in one year by labor and property located in the United States, regardless of who owns the resources.[1] GDP is the summary statistic that comes from our national income and product accounts (NIPA) compiled by the Bureau of Economic Analysis (BEA) in the U.S. Department of Commerce. The NIPA and its components are the most exhaustive statistical collection efforts ever undertaken and collectively give us our most comprehensive view of the economy's performance.

The need to know more about the economy became apparent during the Great Depression of the 1930s when it was discovered that our information about overall economic performance was limited at best. Pioneering work on GDP and the national income accounts was done by Dr. Simon Kuznets in the early 1930s who later received the Nobel Prize for his efforts. The measure has been continually refined and improved since then, and in December of 1999, the U.S. Department of Commerce announced that the development of GDP and NIPA was "its achievement of the century."[2]

---

[1] In 1991, GDP replaced *gross national product (GNP)*, a measure of the total income produced in one year with labor and property supplied by U.S. residents, regardless of where the resources are located. The conversion to GDP made the measurement of total output consistent with the system of accounts used by the World Bank and most other industrial nations.

[2] "GDP: One of the Great Inventions of the 20th Century," *Survey of Current Business*, January 2000.

Estimating GDP

The concept of GDP is fairly easy to grasp. Basically, all we have to do is find out how many goods, services, and structures are produced in a year, multiply them by their prices, and then add them up to get a dollar measure of GDP. This is how the $14,075.5 billion, or $14.1 trillion, in Table 2-1(A) was derived and this was the first GDP number reported by the BEA for 2009.

However, the size and complexity of any economy makes this simple computation a monumental task. It is so difficult, in fact, that it is more accurate to say that GDP is "estimated" rather than measured. So, exactly where do economists start when it comes to estimating the size of our GDP?

Perhaps the most useful information is published every five years in the form of an economic census that covers more than seven million U.S. businesses. The most recent census appeared in 2007 and covers more than 95 percent of GDP expenditures. The "best-level" information in this report helps the BEA estimate the vast majority of final expenditures made by consumers, businesses, government and members of the international community.

Data from a variety of other sources are also used to supplement the underlying five-year estimates. For example, income is derived from the Quarterly Census of Employment and Wages that is conducted by the Bureau of Labor Statistics (BLS). This report covers more than 98 percent of U.S. jobs and provides income data from wages, salaries, stock options and even executive bonuses. In addition, the Internal Revenue Service provides estimates for corporate profits; the Census Bureau conducts retail trade surveys to update shifts in consumer spending patterns; and, the Customs Bureau provides other data on exports and imports.

Other GDP entries, as in the case of owner-occupied housing, have to be imputed. For example, someone who rents an apartment makes a periodic payment to cover the value of housing services received, whereas the owner of a home does not. To accurately reflect the value of all housing services in GDP, the BEA imputes the rental value of owner-occupied housing.

There are many more examples, but the bottom line is that the estimation of GDP is a complex undertaking. And, as GDP estimates get farther from the most recent "best-level" economic census, the need to "benchmark" or realign GDP estimates with the next five-year economic census becomes more pronounced.[3] The result is a series of GDP reports that starts a single quarterly estimate of annual performance. Then, as new source data become available from the Census, BLS, IRS and other agencies, the quarterly estimate is revised twice more. Annual revisions to the revised quarterly estimates then follow, and finally five-year revisions, or benchmarks, are made to reflect the newest economic census.

Table 2-1
Computation of GDP in Current *and* Constant (Chained) Dollars

(A) GDP in Current Prices (billions of dollars):

Annual Domestic Output		Quantity in millions	Current Prices	Value in billions of $
Goods:	Automobiles	7	$30,000	$210.0
	Chairs	5	80	4.0
	..... Other	–	–	–
Services:	Legal	8	550	4.4
	Child care/wk	3	100	0.3
	..... Other	–	–	–
Structures:	Residential	1.4	140,000	196.0
	Commercial	1	340,000	340.0
	..... Other	–	–	–
	GDP in current dollars			*$14,075.5*

(B) Real or Constant GDP (in chained 2000 dollars):

Annual Domestic Output		Quantity in millions	2000 Dollars	Value in billions of $
Goods:	Automobiles	7	$20,000	$140.0
	Chairs	5	100	0.1
	..... Other	–	–	–
Services:	Legal	8	412	3.3
	Child care/wk	3	60	0.2
	..... Other	–	–	–
Structures:	Residential	1.4	114,740	160.6
	Commercial	1	69,469	269.5
	..... Other	–	–	–
	GDP in constant dollars			*$11,340.9*

---

[3] An excellent discussion of these issues can be found at: Landfeld, Seskin, and Fraumeni, "Taking the Pulse of the Economy: Measuring GDP," *Journal of Economic Perspectives*, Vol. 22, No. 2, Spring 2008.

These revisions mean that we never have the luxury of just adding the latest GDP numbers to an existing time series such as that shown in Figure 2-2 on page 25. Instead, we always have to obtain the most recent estimates for the whole series regardless of whether our interest is in long-term trends or simply in changes from one month to the next.[4]

How Reliable Are the Revisions?

The revisions that are the most apparent to GDP users are the monthly revisions of the quarterly estimates, which are made as new data become available. The BEA in the U.S. Department of Commerce releases three estimates according to the following:

Advance – released near the end of the *first* month after the end of the quarter.
Preliminary – released near end of the *second* month after end of the quarter.
Final – released near the end of the *third* month after the end of the quarter.

Figure 2-1 shows the three GDP estimates from the third quarter of 2007 through the first quarter of 2009. Each quarterly estimate is reported on an annualized basis—which means that this is the rate at which the economy would grow for a twelve-month period if the growth in the other three quarters were the same as the current one. Since this is seldom the case, the final figures for the year will be slightly different.

Despite the frequent revisions, they provide surprisingly reliable results. A BEA study found that each of the estimates— advance, preliminary, and final—provide reliable indications of the *direction* of real GDP change 97 percent of the time. In addition, they provide reliable indications of the *rate* of change (accelerating or decelerating rates of growth) about 75 percent of the time.[5]

In addition, the size of the monthly revision is usually not very large when compared to the advance estimate, the first estimate made

---

[4] To illustrate, a 1999 benchmark revision was made to treat software purchases as a capital investment, rather than to treat it as a business expense. This revision caused an increase in the level of GDP that extended back to 1959.
[5] See Dennis J. Fixler, and Bruce T. Grimm, "Reliability of GDP and Related NIPA Estimates," *Survey of Current Business*, January 2002. The survey covered a 68-quarter period beginning in 1983 and ending in 2000.

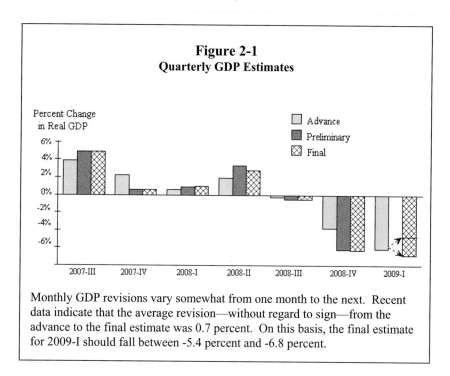

Figure 2-1
Quarterly GDP Estimates

Monthly GDP revisions vary somewhat from one month to the next. Recent data indicate that the average revision—without regard to sign—from the advance to the final estimate was 0.7 percent. On this basis, the final estimate for 2009-I should fall between -5.4 percent and -6.8 percent.

for the quarter. In fact, on average, the final revision falls within +/- 0.7 percent of the advance estimate. When all of these factors are taken into account, it turns out that the advance estimate for any given quarter—despite the fact that it is revised almost continually—is a fairly reliable statistic.

Current vs. Constant Dollar or Real GDP

So far we have covered some of the issues that relate to getting a reasonable estimate of GDP at a given point in time. For the most part, if current prices are used, then the measure is simply *GDP*, or *GDP in current prices* and is the measure illustrated in part A of Table 2-1.

However, there are often times when we want to compare the GDP in one period with the GDP in another. This is easily done, but first we have to recognize that prices are likely to change over time, and that these price changes will bias the resulting comparison. As a result, economists have introduced the concept of "real GDP" to remove these price distortions.

Whenever we see the term "real" or "constant dollar" measures being used, the BEA has simply recomputed GDP using a constant set of base-year prices. Right now this is done with prices as they existed in year 2000, but they too will eventually be updated as time goes on. The advantage of this procedure is that if GDP is computed for two different periods, and if the same prices are used to value the output in both periods, then any difference between the two GDP amounts *must* be due to changes in the quantity of goods, services and structures produced—the difference cannot be due to price changes. So when a fixed set of year 2000 base-year prices is used, the measure is called *real GDP*, or *GDP in constant (2000) dollars*—even though there is nothing otherwise "real" about the computation.

Table 2-1 illustrates both types of computations for the U.S. economy in the first quarter of 2009 (sometimes denoted 2009-I). Suppose that the items in the quantity column represent actual amounts produced in that year. If output is valued at prices that existed at that time, the total value of production—or GDP in current dollars—is taking place at an annual rate of $14,075.5 billion. In the bottom part of the table, the same output is computed using smaller 2000 chain weighted prices to give us a value of $11,340.9 billion.[6]

---

[6] The actual statistical method—i.e., "chain-weighted" or "chained-linked" prices—used for constant dollar prices is a bit more complex than the discussion here, but the result is the same. In the first quarter of 1996, the U.S. Department of Commerce switched from a system of 1987 fixed-weight prices to a chain-linked set of prices because some prices were changing relatively more than other prices over time. This was especially true for desk-top computers which had declined an average of 13 percent annually since 1987.

To illustrate, suppose that X number of computers were made in 1987 at an average price of Y, resulting in a contribution to GDP of XY (X times Y). If we jump ahead ten years and let X' represent the number of computers made in 1997 (hundreds, if not thousands, of times as many as in 1987), and if they are valued at the average computer price, Y, that prevailed in 1987, then the dollar value computer component (X'Y) of GDP would be overstated. An alternative approach would be to adjust the average cost of computers downward by an average of 13 percent annually to a point where the average 1997 price was Y', so that the GDP contribution in that year amounts to X'Y'.

The phrase "chain-weighted" or "chain-linked" refers to the manner in which percentage increases are computed from one year to the next. For example, under the old method, prices from an earlier year were used to value output that was produced in a later period. Under the new method, the weighting is done with prices from both years using a geometric mean that economists call the "Fisher Ideal." A brief numerical example of this computation also appears in the Appendix at the end of this book.

Total GDP in constant dollars is smaller because the year 2000 prices in the middle column are less than prices in 2009.[7]

The advantage of using constant dollar prices is that it enables us to compare the annual rate of total output in the first quarter of 2009 to the third quarter of 2005, or to any other year and quarter for that matter. So if real GDP, or GDP in constant dollars, changed by 2 or 3 percent, the difference must be due to changes in the number of goods, services, and/or structures produced after compensating for changes in price levels. The increase *cannot* be due to inflation.

Does GDP Overlook Anything?

You bet! For example, GDP tells us nothing about the mix, or composition of output. A bigger real or constant dollar GDP only tells us that the dollar value of total output increased. We don't know if the increase was due to the production of new roads, homes, parks and libraries—or to the increased production of nerve gas, exotic military defense expenditures, and toxic waste landfills. Also, GDP doesn't tell us anything about the quality of life. For example, you might feel that the quality of life is enhanced every time a city park or museum is built instead of a military combat aircraft.

Perhaps the biggest limitation is that GDP excludes nonmarket activities such as the services performed by homemakers and the services people perform for themselves. For example, GDP will go down if a homeowner marries his or her housekeeper and does not hire a replacement. Likewise, GDP will go up if you hire someone to mow your own yard, but it will not go up if you do it yourself.

Other activities—prostitution, gambling, and drug running—are mostly illegal and are simply not reported to the IRS, Department of Commerce, or to anyone else. These activities are part of the underground economy and are not directly included in GDP, although estimates have been made for their inclusion.[8]

---

[7] Whenever a series is expressed in "real" terms, only the *percentage change* is relevant, not the dollar or index value of the series. When we focus on percentage changes, the choice of the base year is not important.

[8] In December 1985, GNP statistics extending back to 1929 were revised upward to account for the unreported underground economy activity. As a result of the revision, GNP in 1984 went up by $119.9 billion, and these revisions are now part of GDP. Even so, some private sector economists think that these revisions were not large enough.

GDP—A Measure of Output or Welfare?

Occasionally GDP is criticized on the grounds that it does not adequately measure our welfare, or our overall feeling of well-being. Do increases in GDP mean that we are really better off one might ask—especially during times of urban sprawl, environmental congestion, high divorce rates, and so on?[9] The short answer is that no single series could ever be comprehensive enough to take into account all of the factors that make us happy or unhappy. However, there is some truth to the assertion that GDP is at least a partial measure of welfare.

We can say this because a market economy is based on voluntary transactions. For example, whenever you buy something that was just produced (a transaction reflected in GDP), you must have felt that the money you gave up was worth less to you than the product you acquired—otherwise you would not have made the transaction. Likewise, the producer must have felt that the product given up was worth less than the money received—or the producer would not have made the sale. In the end, the exchange took place because both parties felt that they were better off after the transaction than they were before it took place.

Even so, we need to remember that GDP was designed as a measure of total output, not as an overall measure of welfare—so those who claim that it fails in this regard really miss the mark. The fact that GDP can tell us anything about welfare should be considered as a plus, and we should be looking at the glass as if it were half full rather than half empty.

Gross National Happiness

Still, some people want to have a more comprehensive measure of welfare or happiness, and so we take note here of the official efforts by the government of Bhutan to establish a measure of Gross National Happiness (GNH), which they prefer to GDP.[10] While their statistics are in the early stages of development, they cover many traditional

---

[9] This argument is made by Cobb, Halstead, and Rowe, "If the GDP is Up, Why is America Down?" *Atlantic Monthly*, October, 1995.

[10] The websites at www.grossnationalhappiness.com and www.bhutanstudies.org.bt report on these efforts. GNH is reported on a scale from 0 to 1, with a score of 1.0 being perfect happiness.

economic measures such as household income and home ownership along with many other non-economic variables. For example, one of the components of GNH is the frequency of meditation (psychological wellbeing), another is the perception of soil erosion and river pollution (ecology), and yet another is the long-term disability status and body mass indices (health) to name just a few.

Other components of GNH include the "ability to understand lozey"—a rich oral poetic composition tradition—and "Zorig chusum skills"—the thirteen visual arts that the Bhutanese have practiced for generations. These components are culturally biased, of course, and that makes international comparisons of GNH difficult, but they seem to work for the Bhutanese, which is one reason the GNH statistics were established in the first place.

One of the Great Inventions of the 20th Century

Economists, as you can tell by now, are passionate about their work, and they are passionate about their statistics, especially GDP and the national income and product accounts that support it. This endeavor is truly one of the remarkable efforts of our time, and the recognition the U.S. Department of Commerce bestowed on these efforts is well deserved. GDP truly is "one of the great inventions of the 20th century."

Gross Domestic Product

Compiled by:	Bureau of Economic Analysis in the U.S. Department of Commerce
Frequency:	Quarterly with two subsequent monthly revisions
Release date:	*Advance* estimate at the end of the first month following end of the quarter
Revisions:	*Preliminary* estimate the end of the second month; *Final* revision at the end of the third month following end of the quarter; *Annual* revision every July; *Comprehensive* benchmark revision every 5 years
Internet:	http://www.bea.gov/ http://EconSources.com

Recession vs. Depression

We generally want to know more than the size of GDP at any given time—we also want to see how it changes over time. The reason is that GDP does not always go up—it sometimes goes down as it did during 2008-09.

Over time, successive contractions and expansions of GDP are sometimes called *business cycles*—which implies systematic changes in real GDP marked by alternating periods of expansion and contraction. Other economists prefer to talk of *business fluctuations*, which imply alternating, but not systematic, periods of contraction and expansion.

When Is the Economy in a Recession?

That depends on the measure as two different definitions are used to address this question.

For example, the first definition has a recession occurring whenever real GDP (or GDP measured in constant dollars) declines for two consecutive quarters. This definition is popular because GDP is reported on a regular basis and it is fairly easy to keep track of changes in the quarterly GDP estimates.

The second—and ultimately official—definition is not from the Bureau of Economic Analysis, the Department of Commerce, or any other government agency. Instead, it comes from the National Bureau of Economic Research (NBER), a prestigious private institute with a long and distinguished record of research into the cause and measurement of business cycles.[11] According to the NBER, a recession is defined as "a significant decline in activity spread across the economy, lasting more than a few months, visible in industrial

---

[11] A current list of the seven prominent economists who make up the NBER's business cycle dating committee can be found at http://www.nber.org. Also see "Determination of the December 2007 Peak in Economic Activity" article at the NBER (December 11, 2008) for more on this topic.

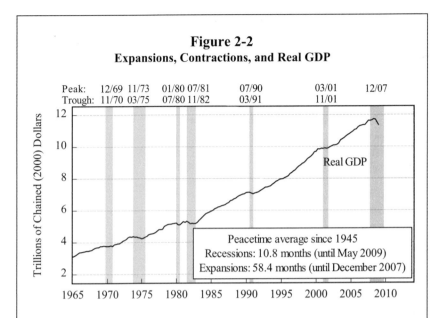

Figure 2-2
Expansions, Contractions, and Real GDP

The shaded areas in the figure represent recessions which can be of varying lengths. According to the NBER, the U.S. economy entered the last recession in December 2007. When this book went to press in May of 2009, it was clear that the recession would be the longest and deepest since the 1930s even though it had not yet ended. While the recession appears to have ended in late 2009 in the above figure this is only an approximation on the part of the authors.

production, employment, real income, and wholesale-retail sales."[12] When shown graphically in Figure 2-2, recessions appear shaded and the expansions that follow are unshaded. Together, a recession and an expansion make up a business cycle.

To nail down the turning points of the business cycle, the NBER considers as much data as it can—most of it monthly—and then identifies specific months (rather than quarters) when the economy reached a relative peak or trough in economic activity. As a result, the NBER turning points may not always coincide with quarterly changes in real GDP. However, the prestige of the NBER is such that virtually all economists use the two-quarter definition of a recession only until the NBER announces the "official" business cycle turning points, which are also shown in Table 2-2.

---

[12] "The NBER's Recession Dating Procedure," April 10, 2003, http://www.nber.org.

Table 2-2
Business Cycle Expansions and Contractions in the United States

Peak	Trough	Peak	Duration in Months[*]		
			Recession	Expansion	Cycle
October 1860	June 1861	April 1865	8	_46_	_54_
April 1865	December 1867	June 1869	_32_	18	_50_
June 1869	December 1870	October 1873	18	34	52
October 1873	March 1879	March 1882	65	36	101
March 1882	May 1885	March 1887	38	22	60
March 1887	April 1888	July 1890	13	27	40
July 1890	May 1891	January 1893	10	20	30
January 1893	June 1894	December 1895	17	18	35
December 1895	June 1897	June 1899	18	24	42
June 1899	December 1900	September 1902	18	21	39
September 1902	August 1904	May 1907	23	33	56
May 1907	June 1908	January 1910	13	19	32
January 1910	January 1912	January 1913	24	12	36
January 1913	December 1914	August 1918	23	_44_	_67_
August 1918	March 1919	January 1920	_7_	10	_17_
January 1920	July 1921	May 1923	18	22	40
May 1923	July 1924	October 1926	14	27	41
October 1926	November 1927	August 1929	13	21	34
August 1929	March 1933	May 1937	43	50	93
May 1937	June 1938	February 1945	13	_80_	_93_
February 1945	October 1945	November 1948	_8_	37	_45_
November 1948	October 1949	July 1953	11	_45_	_56_
July 1953	May 1954	August 1957	_10_	39	_49_
August 1957	April 1958	April 1960	8	24	32
April 1960	February 1961	December 1969	10	_106_	_116_
December 1969	November 1970	November 1973	_11_	36	_47_
November 1973	March 1975	January 1980	16	58	74
January 1980	July 1980	July 1981	6	12	18
July 1981	November 1982	July 1990	16	92	108
July 1990	March 1991	March 2001	8	120	128
March 2001	November 2001	December 2007	8	73	81
December 2007	--	--	--		

Averages for peacetime cycles (recession and expansion) only:[*]

	1854-1991 (27 cycles)		18	33	52
	1854-1919 (14 cycles)		22	24	47
	1919-1945 (5 cycles)		20	26	45
	1945-2003 (10 cycles)		10	52	

*Cycles are measured from peak-to-peak and the underscored figures are for wartime periods.
Source: National Bureau of Economic Research and the *Survey of Current Business.*

An advantage of the NBER approach is that monthly data are subject to less frequent revision than are the GDP numbers compiled by the BEA. A disadvantage is that many months may pass before the NBER makes an official announcement. For example, the NBER took 8 months to declare that the 2001 recession had begun, and then another 20 months to decide that it was officially over. In November 2008 it took 11 months for the NBER to decide that the economy had entered recession in December 2007. Delays like this are partially responsible for the popularity of the first definition.

In addition to the delays, the two approaches sometimes appear to be out of synch. For example, when the NBER declared in December of 2008 that a recession had begun a year earlier, real GDP had declined in only one of the three previous quarters. An upcoming annual or five-year benchmark revision of GDP may change some of the 2008 estimates so that they better conform to the NBER's recession dates, but clearly problems like this make it more difficult to pinpoint precisely where we are at any given time.

What About A Depression?

It is difficult to give an exact definition of a depression because the U.S. economy experienced only one since 1865, and that was the Great Depression that began with the stock market crash in October of 1929 and ended in 1939. The NBER even divides this period into two shorter declines as can be seen in Table 2-2.

Even so, the extent of decline in the 1930s was extraordinary, and recessions both before and after never reached the extremes of production decline, joblessness, and price deflation that we experienced in the 1930s. More modern contractions, such as those shown in Figure 2-2, were so mild that real GDP barely seems to decline at all, despite all of the attention paid to them in the media.

Of course some observers might argue that we still have yet to see the full extent of GDP decline in the 2008-09 recession, but most economists are relatively confident that the extreme conditions of the 1930s will not return anytime soon. Forecasts like this, as we argued in Chapter 1, can be notoriously wrong but we'll take our chances and side with those who basically expect a recession of record length—perhaps depth—but not a depression.

The NIPAs

The National Income and Product Accounts, or NIPAs, are a comprehensive set of nearly 300 accounts that provide detailed information on our nation's income and output. GDP is the best-known NIPA measure and is treated as the sum of the final expenditures of four sectors—consumers, private businesses, government, and a conceptual "rest of the world" sector to capture the net exports of goods and services.

The approach of dividing the economy into sectors and then aggregating each of the sectors to get GDP is evident in Table 2-3, which presents the advance estimate for the 2009-I quarter. The table also shows the size of each component in current dollar and constant (2000) dollar amounts as well as the relative size of each in percentage terms.

Are Other Statistics Related to GDP?

Good question! In fact, the very structure of the NIPAs almost guarantees that the majority of economic statistics are related to GDP one way or another. Some statistics report on the various components of total output—goods, services, structures—that are shown in Table 2-1. Other series track subcategories like durable and nondurable goods, and even others are used to track the production of various product categories like automobiles and residential housing.

Many statistics, including most of those examined in this book, are designed to track GDP or one of its major components, while other statistics are designed to help predict future changes in the level of GDP or its major components. In addition, whenever anything is produced, income is generated in the form of wages, tips, salaries, interest, rents, and profits. Since the recipients eventually spend this income, even more statistics are kept on these activities. Almost every economic statistic, then, is related to GDP in one way or another.

Table 2-3
The National Income and Product Accounts
First Quarter 2009 Advanced Estimates—Billions of Dollars

	Current	Constant (2000$)	% GDP
Gross domestic product	*$14,075.5*	*$11,340.9*	*100.0*
Personal consumption expenditures	*9,955.7*	*8,214.2*	*70.7*
Durable goods	963.8	1,133.9	6.8
Nondurable goods	2,810.8	2,326.2	20.0
Services	6,181.1	4,746.5	43.9
Gross private domestic investment	*1,579.8*	*1,329.8*	*11.2*
Fixed investment	1,716.6	1,444.3	12.2
Nonresidential	1,332.4	1,190.6	9.5
Structures	487.2	293.9	3.5
Equipment and software	845.1	875.3	6.0
Residential	384.2	294.2	2.7
Change in private inventories	-136.8	-103.7	-1.0
Net exports of goods and services	*-337.7*	*-308.4*	*-2.4*
Exports	1,536.7	1,331.0	10.9
Imports	1,874.4	1,639.5	13.3
Government consumption & gross investment	*2,877.7*	*2,073.8*	*20.4*
Federal	1,102.5	816.1	7.8
National defense	749.0	545.9	5.3
Nondefense	353.5	269.8	2.5
State and local	1,775.2	1,259.7	12.6
Residual		*7.3*	

Source: *Bureau of Economic Analysis*. The first column of numbers shows current dollar entries, the second column shows "real" or constant dollar entries that are based on the chain weighting calculations discussed the Appendix. Also, note that one of the idiosyncrasies of chain weighting is that "real" or constant dollar amounts are sometimes larger, and sometimes smaller, than their corresponding current dollar amounts—as a result, a residual is employed because chain weighted numbers cannot be added. The percent of GDP column is based on current dollars; percentages are slightly different for chain weighted dollars.

If there is a difficulty with the above table, it is that the numbers are so large as to boggle the mind. As a result, the BEA also presents another popular table that shows the contribution to the change in real GDP made by individual GDP components (see Table 2-4 on the next page). To illustrate, this table shows that real GDP decreased at an annual rate of 6.1 percent in the first quarter of 2009. This decrease was due to the -8.83 percent change in private domestic investment expenditures and the -0.81 percent change in government expenditures, but was offset by the 1.50 percent increase in personal consumption expenditures and the 1.99 percent increase in net export of goods and services—all of which combine to give us the -6.1 percent change in real GDP.

Table 2-4
Contributions to Percent Change in Real GDP
Percent Change at Annual Rates—Advance First Quarter 2009 Estimate

	2008-II	2008-III	2008-IV	2009-I
Gross domestic product	*2.8*	*-0.5*	*-6.3*	*-6.1*
Personal consumption expenditures	*0.87*	*-2.75*	*-2.99*	*1.50*
Durable goods	-0.21	-1.16	-1.67	0.61
Nondurable goods	0.80	-1.57	-1.97	0.26
Services	0.28	-0.03	0.66	0.63
Gross private domestic investment	*-1.74*	*0.6*	*-3.47*	*-8.83*
Fixed investment	-0.25	-0.79	-3.36	-6.04
Nonresidential	0.27	-0.19	-2.56	-4.68
Structures	0.64	0.36	-0.38	-2.13
Equipment and software	-0.37	-0.55	-2.18	-2.55
Residential	-0.52	-0.60	-0.80	-1.36
Change in private inventories	-1.50	0.84	-0.11	-2.79
Net exports of goods and services	*2.93*	*1.05*	*-0.15*	*1.99*
Exports	1.54	0.40	-3.44	-4.06
Imports	1.39	0.65	3.29	6.05
Government consumption & gross investment	*0.78*	*1.14*	*0.26*	*-0.81*
Federal	0.47	0.97	0.52	-0.32
National defense	0.36	0.85	0.18	-0.38
Nondefense	0.11	0.12	0.34	0.03
State and local	0.31	0.17	-0.25	-0.49

Source: Table 1.1.2, first quarter advanced GDP estimates, Bureau of Economic Analysis.

  The advantage of the above table is that it helps us see where the major weaknesses in the economy are. For example, if we look at the four quarters shown in the table above, it is clear that declines in fixed investment, as well declines in personal consumption expenditures for durable and nondurable goods, were largely responsible for the overall decline in GDP.

Personal Income

Personal income sounds as if it should refer to the income people earn: their salaries, tips, and hourly wages. In a way it does, but in a more fundamental sense, *personal income* (*PI*) represents the total current income received by persons from all sources *minus* social insurance payments. Another key measure is **disposable personal income** (**DPI**), the amount we have left to spend after taxes and non-tax payments.

GDP may be the primary measure of the nation's total output, but it is not the best measure of the nation's income for two reasons. First, GDP *includes* output generated with resources owned by foreign residents. Since income earned by these individuals leaves the United States, it cannot be included as part of our nation's income. Second, GDP *ignores* income earned by U.S. residents as a result of their investments abroad.

Table 2-5
Converting GDP to GNP, Billions of Current Dollars

Gross domestic product (GDP)	**$14,264.6**
Plus: Income receipts earned abroad	798.3
Less: Income payments to foreign residents	665.1
Gross national product (GNP)	**14,397.8**

Data are annual for 2008

Table 2-5 shows the two adjustments necessary to convert GDP (the measure of total domestic output) to GNP (the measure of total income).[13] The first step is to add the income earned by U.S. residents as a result of their international investments. However, because this data are not available for the advance quarter estimate, the data in the

---

[13] In the case of the U.S., the two adjustments are nearly offsetting, so that GNP and GDP are almost the same. This is not always the case for other countries. For example, Canada's GDP is several percentage points larger than its GNP because the foreign investment in Canada was much larger than Canadian investments in the rest of the world.

table are for 2008. The second step is to subtract the income earned by foreign residents as a result of their investments in the United States.[14]

The rest of the NIPA components are shown in Figure 2-3. To go from GNP of $14,397.8 billion to a *net national product* (*NNP*) of $12,565.5 billion, we subtract the wear and tear on the capital stock, which is more formally known as *consumption of fixed capital.* The government then takes a slice of the income earned by businesses in the form of indirect business taxes and the remainder, called *national income* (*NI*), is $12,429.7 billion. This represents the sum of employee compensation, proprietors' income, rental income, corporate profits, and net interest payments in the economy.

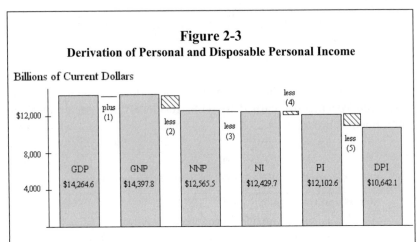

Figure 2-3
Derivation of Personal and Disposable Personal Income

Billions of Current Dollars

	GDP	GNP	NNP	NI	PI	DPI
	$14,264.6	$14,397.8	$12,565.5	$12,429.7	$12,102.6	$10,642.1

Note: data are annual for 2008
(1) Factor income payments to foreigners are subtracted, and factor income receipts from foreign residents are added to GDP to get gross national product (GNP).
(2) Consumption of fixed capital is subtracted from GNP to get net national product (NNP).
(3) Indirect business taxes are subtracted from NNP to get national income (NI).
(4) Undistributed corporate profits and social insurance payments are subtracted and transfer payments are added to NI to get personal income (PI).
(5) Tax and nontax payments are subtracted from PI to get disposable personal income (DPI).

To get to *personal income* (*PI*), undistributed corporate profits (retained earnings) and contributions for social insurance payments

---

[14] Because of these adjustments, it takes longer to obtain GNP estimates. Because this book went to press when only the advance data were available for the first quarter of 2009, the data in Table 2-5 and Figure 2-3 are annual for 2008.

like social security are subtracted. At the same time, transfer payments, such as unemployment compensation, welfare, and other aid, are added in. The result, shown in Figure 2-3, is the aggregate measure called personal income in the amount of $12,102.6 billion.

Finally, if we subtract tax and other nontax payments from PI, we get a ***disposable personal income (DPI)*** of $10,642.1 billion, the income people actually have left over for spending purposes.

Personal Income as an Economic Indicator

We could plot personal income to see what it looks like, but first we would like to talk about its stability. For example, if we were to examine the nominal (unadjusted for inflation) personal income series from 1965 until the first quarter of 2009, a period of 531 months, we would see that it only turned down a total of 28 times, and just 13 of those declines were during a recession.

We could examine PI in real terms, but we could also examine the next income measure in the NIPA, which is DPI. After all, this is the money that we have available to us for spending, so we should be able relate to it better than we can to an abstract NIPA category like national income or personal income. And, it would be even more meaningful if we could examine DPI in real terms so that inflation does not distort the real picture.

Figure 2-4 on the next page shows DPI in both nominal and real (chained 2000) dollars from 1965 until the first quarter of 2009.[15] Overall the constant dollar or inflation-adjusted series appears to rise modestly during expansions and be relatively flat to modestly negative during recessions. In retrospect, this is exactly the pattern we should have expected. Disposable personal income is such a large component of GDP (about 75 percent in the first quarter of 2009) that we would expect both to go up and down together even though the monthly movements are relatively small. In fact, DPI would have been down a little more during the recessions had it not been for transfer payments that act as buffers to lessen the decline.

---

[15] Personal income data are collected and published both monthly and quarterly. The monthly data are released in BEA's "Personal Income and Outlays" news release. Quarterly estimates for personal income are published in the *Survey of Current Business* along with other NIPA accounts.

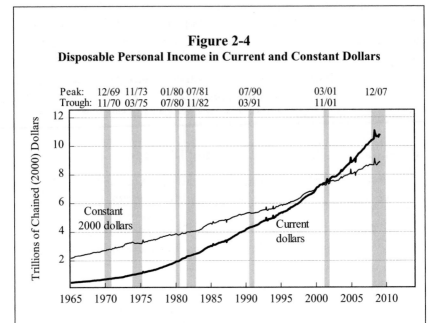

Figure 2-4
Disposable Personal Income in Current and Constant Dollars

| Peak: | 12/69 11/73 | 01/80 07/81 | 07/90 | 03/01 | 12/07 |
| Trough: | 11/70 03/75 | 07/80 11/82 | 03/91 | 11/01 | |

Disposable personal income is fairly stable and often goes up even during most recessions, although the most recent one may be an exception because of its severity. The constant dollar measure is preferred by economists, although the the current dollar measure is the one most frequently reported in the press.

On rare occasions DPI can even be affected by political events. Right after the presidential election of 1992, many individuals who feared higher tax rates under the Clinton administration arranged to have their annual bonuses paid in December of 1992, rather than wait for January when a new tax year—and possibly higher tax rates— would apply.[16] Most economists think that this accounts for part of the $155 billion "spike" in DPI that is visible in Figure 2-4.

What Else Should We Know About Personal Income?

First, because PI and DPI are such large and relatively constant components of GDP, they behave more as coincident indicators than

---

[16] Under the Clinton administration, Congress made the individual income tax more progressive by adding a fourth marginal tax bracket of 39.6 percent which applied to taxable income over $250,000.

as leading or lagging ones. Coincident indicators don't give us the advance warning of where the economy is heading that leading indicators do, but they are nevertheless important because they tell us where we are and how well we are doing.

Also, we should note that although personal income is one of the national income and product account components, it is also available as a monthly statistic. However, it is also subject to the same revisions as GDP, so any new monthly announcement of personal income will almost always mention a revision of the previous monthly figure.

Finally, we should note that real (constant) dollar estimates are almost always a better measure of how we are doing because they remove the distortions caused by inflation. The BEA releases both real (measured in chained dollars) and current dollar estimates simultaneously, but the press often focuses on the current dollar figures because the amounts are larger.

Personal and Disposable Personal Income

Indicator status:	Coincident economic indicator overall
Compiled by:	Bureau of Economic Analysis
Frequency:	Monthly
Release date:	End of month for the previous month
Revisions:	Preliminary and final revisions of the advance estimates
Published data:	*Economic Indicators*, Council of Economic Advisors
	Survey of Current Business, U.S. Department of Commerce
	Personal Income and Outlays, BEA News Release, U.S. Department of Commerce
Internet:	http://www.bea.gov
	http://www.EconSources.com

Chapter 3

PRODUCTION and GROWTH

Purchasing Managers' Index

Economists have long been interested in predicting the output of goods, and one of the more interesting indicators of this activity is the monthly *purchasing managers' index* (*PMI*) compiled by the Institute for Supply Management (ISM).[1] The series is reliable as both a *coincident* and a *leading* indicator—meaning that it tells us where the economy is and where it is going. It is one of a handful of major series maintained by a private industry and/or educational group rather than a division in the U.S. Department of Commerce.[2]

The PMI is the major component of the ISM's monthly Report on Business® which surveys manufacturing firms on a number of topics including production, new orders, inventories of purchased materials, employment, and supplier deliveries.[3] The ISM releases the PMI on the first business day following the close of the reporting month.

---

[1] ISM, formerly known as the National Association of Purchasing Management (NAPM), is a not-for-profit association that exists to educate, develop, and advance the purchasing and supply management profession. With more than 40,000 members, ISM and its affiliates work to establish and maintain best-in-class professional standards pertaining to research, education, and certification. For more information, contact ISM Customer Service, 2055 E. Centennial Circle, P.O. Box 22160, Tempe, AZ 85285-2160.

[2] Other series examined in this book include the *help-wanted advertising index* and the *consumer confidence survey* compiled by The Conference Board, the *index of consumer expectations* compiled by the Institute for Social Research at the University of Michigan, the *Dow Jones Industrial Average* compiled by the Dow Jones Corporation, and the *S&P 500* by Standard & Poor's Corporation.

[3] The supplier deliveries series is used by The Conference Board as one of the components of its monthly *index of leading economic indicators*.

The Sample and the Survey

The PMI is derived from a monthly survey of purchasing managers at over 300 companies in approximately 20 industries. Each industry is weighted according to its contribution to GDP, and each firm in the industry is given equal weight, regardless of its size.[4] The questions, such as the one following, are designed to detect changes in the direction and intensity of business activity:[5]

> 9. SUPPLIER DELIVERIES - Check the **ONE** box that best expresses the current month's **OVERALL** delivery performance compared to the previous month.
>
> ☐ **Faster** than   ☐ **Same** as a   ☐ **Slower** than
>   a month ago   month ago   a month ago

When all of the responses are collected, the results are tabulated and then reported in the form of a diffusion index.

What Does a Diffusion Index Tell Us?

A diffusion index is different from other series in that it focuses on the direction and magnitude of change as opposed to the absolute level of the series. The index ranges from 0 to 100 percent and is considered to be expanding whenever it has a value greater than 50 percent, so the more the number exceeds 50 percent, the more intense the expansion of the series. By the same token, the series is contracting when the index is less than 50 percent—so the smaller the number, the more intense the contraction.[6]

In addition to the series on supplier deliveries, separate indices are constructed for production, new orders, inventories of purchased materials, and employment. These five series are combined to make up the overall purchasing management index.[7]

---

[4] Bretz, Robert J., "Behind the Economic Indicators of the NAPM Report on Business," July 1990, in NAPM's *Report on Business Information Kit*, March 2000.

[5] ISM calls the series "supplier deliveries"; BEA calls it "vendor performance."

[6] To illustrate, weights of 1, 0.5, and 0 are given to each of the three responses above. If half of the respondents select "faster" and if half respond "slower," the index will have a value of 50 percent [or, $0.5(1) + 0.5(0) = 0.5$]. Likewise, if 60 percent respond "faster," 20 percent "same," and 20 percent "slower," the index will have a value of 70 percent [or, $0.6(1) + 0.2(0.5) + 0.2(0) = 0.7$]. Any score for this question greater than 0.5 would indicate that the manufacturing side of the economy is expanding.

[7] The weights vary, with new orders having the most importance.

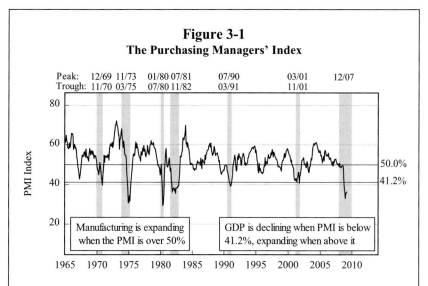

Figure 3-1
The Purchasing Managers' Index

Whenever the PMI is over 50 percent, the manufacturing sector of the economy is expanding. Whenever the PMI is greater than 41.2 percent, the overall economy—which includes services in addition to manufactured goods—is expanding. Because the PMI is a diffusion index, it has the properties of a leading indicator, reaching a peak before the economy peaks and a trough before the economy reaches a trough.

The Historical Record

Figure 3-1 shows the PMI since 1965. The manufacturing sector of the economy is claimed to be generally expanding when the index is above 50 percent, and contracting when below that level. The horizontal line at 41.2 percent is the value of the index thought to be most consistent with no change in real GDP, so the overall economy should be expanding when the PMI is above 41.2, and contracting when the index is below it.[8]

It also helps to examine the intensity and direction of change as well as the general level of the index. For example, when the index was above 41.2 percent and *rising,* the economy was indeed

---

[8] This number is revised annually because GDP is continually being revised. When the last edition of this book was published in 2001, the number was 42.9 rather than 41.2. Most PMI changes, according to economists who do the annual revisions at the U.S. Department of Commerce, are relatively small, in the range of one or two tenths of a percent.

expanding. Yet, when the index was above 41.2 and *declining,* the economy was beginning to slow and headed for a recession.[9]

The reason for this is that the PMI is a diffusion index, which means that it also has the properties of a leading indicator. If we examine Figure 3-1, we can see that the index peaked, with highly variable lead times, well in advance of every recession. Likewise, the index usually hit a minimum just before the recovery began.[10]

Purchasing Managers' Index	
Indicator status:	The level of the PMI is a coincident indicator; peaks and troughs in the PMI series function more as leading indicators with highly variable lead times
Compiled by:	Institute for Supply Management
Frequency:	Monthly
Release date:	First business day following close of the reporting month
Revisions:	None, responses are raw data and are not changed
Published data:	*Manufacturing Report On Business*, ISM's monthly publication
Internet:	http://www.ism.ws
	http://www.EconSources.com

---

[9] A 1985 paper presented by Theodore S. Torda at the NAPM International Conference and later published in *Purchasing Management* (July 1985, pp. 20-22) states that ". . . monthly data on the NAPM composite index and the Commerce Department's composite of leading economic indicators . . . (both) tend to reach their peaks and troughs before those of the general business cycle." Later in the same paper, the author states that "the NAPM composite index clearly leads the (BEA) coincident index."

Another paper by Alan Raedels, "Forecasting the NAPM Purchasing Managers' Index," in the *Journal of Purchasing and Materials Management* (Fall 1990), concluded that "the PMI can be considered a coincident indicator of the economy."

[10] A peak in the series is analogous to an inflection point in a series that grows first at an increasing and then at a decreasing rate. The trough is analogous to an inflection point for a series that decreases at an increasing and then at a decreasing rate.

Index of Industrial Production

The ***index of industrial production*** is a comprehensive index of industrial activity compiled by the Board of Governors of the Federal Reserve System. Because of the Fed's responsibility for monetary policy, and because of delays in reporting final GDP, the index is designed to give the Fed a quicker reading on the overall health and activity of the manufacturing sector of the economy. The monthly index and released midmonth of the following month.

The overall index is made up over 300 individual series that represent a broad range of industries. The data are collected directly from many sources, including gas and electric utilities, the Bureau of Mines, the Census Bureau, other government agencies, and industry trade associations.[11] After the source data are collected, compiled, and weighted according to the respective industry size, they are expressed as a percentage of 2002 base-year output.

Industrial Production and GDP

Recall that GDP is the sum of all of the goods, services, and structures produced in an economy in one year's time. Industrial production covers the goods portion of GDP and amounts to about 30 percent of total output—with services representing about 60 percent of output and structures the remaining 10 percent.

Industrial production is reported in one of several ways: the first is the *total index*, which is a compilation of all individual indices. The total index is also presented by major market groups—with sub-categories for consumer goods, business equipment, information processing, national defense and space equipment, construction and business supplies—and by major industry groups to highlight activity in the manufacturing, mining, and utilities industries.

---

[11] Oddly enough, the Fed uses some *quarterly* series to compile the *monthly* index of industrial production. Specifically, quarterly data from Dataquest, a private agency, is used to determine real output in the computer industry. The Fed does this by making monthly estimates that are then revised as the quarterly data become available.

What About the Historical Record?

Figure 3-2 shows that the total index of industrial production usually behaves as a coincident indicator, meaning that the peaks and troughs in the series occur at approximately the same time that the economy has its peaks and troughs. This is to be expected, since overall industrial production represents such a large proportion of total GDP.

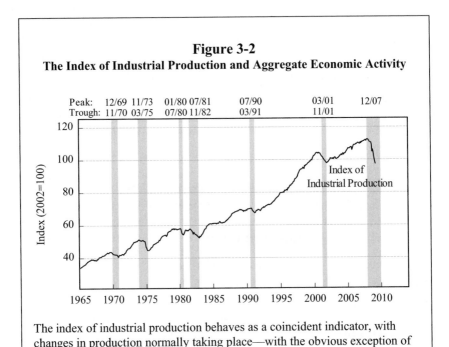

Figure 3-2
The Index of Industrial Production and Aggregate Economic Activity

The index of industrial production behaves as a coincident indicator, with changes in production normally taking place—with the obvious exception of the start of the 2001 recession—at about the same time as changes in the direction of overall economic activity.

When the durable and nondurable goods series are presented separately, as shown in Figure 3-3, it is evident that the durable goods portion of the index is the more volatile component. This normally occurs because the purchase of durable goods—automobiles, boats, furniture, and appliances that last more than three years under normal conditions—can usually be postponed if consumers find themselves short of purchasing power.

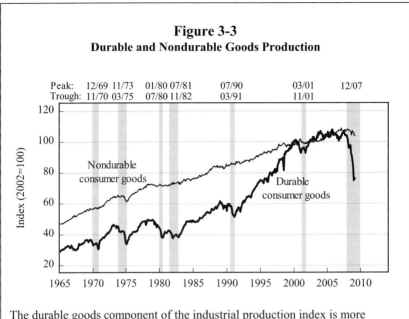

Figure 3-3
Durable and Nondurable Goods Production

The durable goods component of the industrial production index is more volatile than for nondurables. The durables index also performs better as a leading indicator for recessions while the nondurable index is more of a coincident indicator for both recessions and recoveries.

Monthly Estimates and Revisions

The initial release of the index of industrial production, like most other economic data, is subject to considerable revision. The process is complicated by the fact that the overall index is made up of so many different series, most of which become available at separate times, and some of which are themselves subject to further monthly revisions.

The Fed deals with this problem by substituting its own estimates for missing data if data have not yet been received.[12] To illustrate, electric power usage data are not available when the initial report is issued, so the Fed makes a judgment as to what it thinks the

---

[12] See Charles Gilbert, Norman Morin, and Richard Raddock, "Industrial Production and Capacity Utilization: Recent Developments and the 1999 Revision," *Federal Reserve Bulletin*, March 2000.

numbers will be. The same is done for other missing data, so slightly more than half of the initial release is based on the Fed's own estimates. Then, as better data become available over the next three months, it is used in place of the Fed's own estimates.

Despite these procedures, the initial release is fairly reliable. As for revisions, whenever the Fed releases the initial industrial production number for the month, it shows both the previous and the revised estimates for the preceding three months.

Index of Industrial Production

Indicator status:	Overall index generally coincident with changes in real GDP, although the durable goods component is more of a leading indicator for recessions
Compiled by:	Federal Reserve System Board of Governors
Frequency:	Monthly
Release date:	Preliminary estimate around the fifteenth of the following month
Revisions:	Preliminary estimate subject to revision in each of the subsequent 3 months, annual revision every fall for the previous 2 years, benchmark revision every 5 years
Published data:	*Economic Indicators*, Council of Economic Advisors *Statistical Release G.17*, Federal Reserve System
Internet:	http://www.federalreserve.gov http://www.EconSources.com

Capacity Utilization

When the Federal Reserve System collects data on industrial production, it also makes estimates of manufacturing capacity. When the Fed compares the level of industrial production to manufacturing capacity, the result is *capacity utilization*. This monthly series is generally regarded as being a leading economic indicator for downturns in overall economic activity.

Measuring Capacity Utilization

The Fed's data on manufacturing capacity, like its *Index of Industrial Production*, are expressed in terms of an index with a base year of 2002 = 100. The two are then divided to express production as a percentage of actual capacity:

$$\text{Capacity Utilization} = \frac{\text{Index of Industrial Production}}{\text{Index of Industrial Capacity}}$$

In March 2009, for example, the industrial production index stood at 97.4 while the capacity index stood at 122.1. When the former was divided by the latter, capacity utilization was 0.798 or 79.8 percent.

Estimates of industrial capacity are available for a number of industries and product groups, including manufacturing, mining, utilities, durable goods, chemicals, and paper, to name a few. The monthly series is released approximately two weeks after the close of the month and is closely watched by many economists, especially those who watch the Fed.

Why Is Capacity Important to the Fed?

One of the responsibilities of the Fed is to foster steady economic growth in a climate of reasonable price stability. The capacity utilization rate is designed to tell the Fed if the economy is "heating up" to the point where inflation might surge because of production bottlenecks. This sometimes happens when demand for output is so strong that producers are tempted to use less skilled labor and less efficient equipment to generate even more output.

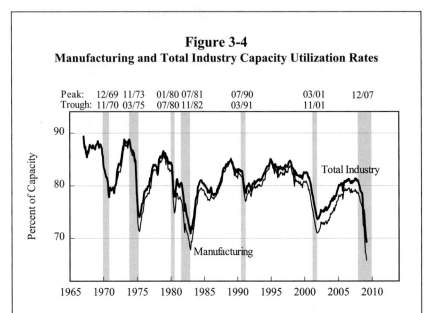

Figure 3-4
Manufacturing and Total Industry Capacity Utilization Rates

Originally, the Fed made capacity utilization estimates for manufacturing. Later, it added mining, utilities, and several others to get a "total industry" series which is now available from 1967 to the present. Despite the availability of the separate "total" series, manufacturing gets most of the attention—although they behave about the same.

When the capacity utilization rate gets high, the Fed might be tempted to tighten the money supply to slow the economy and lessen the threat of inflation. When the capacity utilization rate is low, the economy is perceived to have some "slack" that acts to ease inflationary pressures.

What About the Historical Record?

The capacity utilization rates for two series, manufacturing and total industry, are shown in Figure 3-4. Because the series are expressed as a percent of total capacity, their levels never exceed 100.

Historically, the Bureau of Economic Analysis classified both as leading indicators for peaks (recessions), although the lead times are too variable to be of precise value for forecasting.

The capacity utilization series, like most other economic data, is continually revised as new information becomes available and modifications in data collection and processing are introduced. Because capacity utilization is a ratio of two other series, a revision of either affects the ratio. Consequently, the monthly numbers are revised for up to three months, and the entire series is revised every fall. Finally, a benchmark revision is conducted every five years.

This series is a little different from our other economic indicators in that it is not exclusively intended to forecast changes in future economic activity—but is instead designed as an aid to monetary policy.

Capacity Utilization	
Indicator status:	Leading for recessions; coincident for recoveries
Compiled by:	Federal Reserve System Board of Governors
Frequency:	Monthly
Release date:	Preliminary estimate made midmonth of following month
Revisions:	The preliminary estimate is revised for up to 3 months; annual revisions are targeted for fall, benchmark revisions every 5 years
Published data:	*Economic Indicators*, Council of Economic Advisors *Federal Reserve Bulletin,* Fed Board of Governors *Statistical Release G.17,* Fed Board of Governors
Internet:	http://www.federalreserve.gov/rnd.htm http://www.EconSources.com

Labor Productivity

A key measure of efficiency in the U.S. economy is *output per hour of all persons*, or more commonly known as **labor productivity**. It is published by the Bureau of Labor Statistics and is compiled using both quarterly and monthly data. Several series are released at the same time, with the first one covering the business sector and the second one covering the nonfarm business sector. Because the data are based on quarterly GDP estimates, labor productivity is a quarterly series, although updates are issued monthly.

A third series reporting on manufacturing is also reported by the BLS, but it uses the industrial production indices compiled by the Federal Reserve System. As a result, there can be some variation in the numbers reported at any given time.[13] The business sector series is the most inclusive, but the nonfarm sector is also popular.

How Do We Measure Productivity?

The official BLS definition of business or labor productivity is as follows:

$$\text{Productivity} = \frac{\text{Index of real dollar output}}{\text{Hours of labor input}}$$

The numerator is based on, but is not exactly identical to, the GDP statistics in the national income and product accounts and is measured in real terms so that prices do not distort the dollar value of the output.[14] The denominator is obtained from the BLS Current Employment Statistics (CES) program that provides monthly employment data on payrolls in various industries.[15]

---

[13] In June 2003, the BLS reported revised first quarter productivity data of 2.5 percent for the business sector, 1.9 percent for the nonfarm business sector, and 1.9 percent for the manufacturing sector.

[14] For example, the outputs of general government, nonprofit institutions, paid employees of private households, and the rental value of owner-occupied dwellings are all excluded.

[15] *BLS Handbook of Methods,* Bulletin 2414.

Figure 3-5
Index of Output per Hour of All Persons, Business Sector

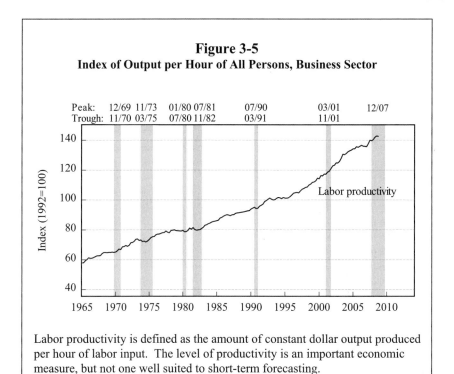

Labor productivity is defined as the amount of constant dollar output produced per hour of labor input. The level of productivity is an important economic measure, but not one well suited to short-term forecasting.

The Historical Record

The historical index shown in Figure 3-5 indicates that productivity has grown slowly but steadily since the late 1950s. The index reached 142.6 in the last quarter of 2008, meaning that workers produced 42.6 percent more output per hour than they did in 1992. When farm workers are removed from the sample the index changes to 141.6, indicating slightly lower productivity in manufacturing.

The index in the figure above appears to exhibit some cyclical behavior, with productivity falling off at the end of most expansions. Most economists think that this occurs because employers tend to hire less skilled and therefore less productive workers when production is high and unemployment rates are low. However, when productivity is expressed as a percentage change from the preceding quarter, as shown in Figure 3-6, it is evident that quarter-to-quarter changes are both volatile and generally unrelated to turning points in real GDP.

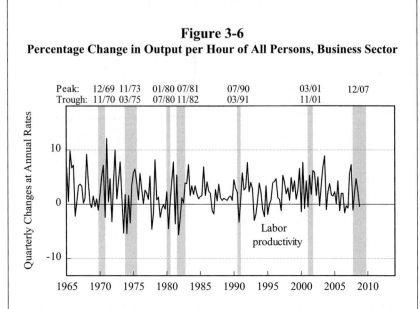

Figure 3-6
Percentage Change in Output per Hour of All Persons, Business Sector

Quarterly changes in labor productivity, a popular way of reporting productivity figures, can be quite dramatic from one quarter to the next. Productivity figures are best thought of as being related to long-term growth; they are unrelated to the turning points in the overall level of economic activity.

Multifactor Productivity

A drawback of labor productivity is that it does not include contributions made by other factors such as capital. Most economists, for example, attribute the spurt in productivity growth during the latter half of the 1990s to the use of the personal computer.

Accordingly, several *multifactor productivity* measures have been developed which relate output to a combination of inputs including labor, capital, energy, and other resources and materials that are used to produce total output. Unfortunately, some of the source data needed to construct such measures are not available quarterly, so the series are only compiled annually. However, even the most recent data for the multifactor series are usually several years old.[16]

---

[16] Even so, the BLS multifactor productivity website at http://www.bls.gov/mfp/ allows you to retrieve annual multifactor productivity data back to 1987.

Labor Productivity in Perspective

Labor productivity measures are useful when we want to explain some of the factors that contribute to long-term economic growth. However, these measures ignore changes in the use of other capital goods like computers. Consequently, any change in the quantity or quality of other resources can make labor seem as if it is more productive than it really is.

Productivity numbers are also slow to be reported because they are constructed using quarterly data from the national income and product accounts. In essence, the quarterly data must first be generated in order for productivity to be computed. Finally, the historical record shows that quarterly productivity numbers have little value as a forecasting tool.

None of this is intended to disparage the series, of course, but we do need to know how the various series are measured and behave if we are to interpret and use them properly.

Labor Productivity

Indicator status:	None
Compiled by:	Bureau of Labor Statistics
Frequency:	Quarterly
Release date:	About 40 days after the close of the quarter
Revisions:	First revisions 30 days after the initial release, additional final revision 60 days after initial release along with initial release of the next quarter estimates
Published data:	*Monthly Labor Review*, U.S. Department of Labor *Economic Indicators*, Council of Economic Advisors
Internet:	http://www.bls.gov/lpc http://www.EconSources.com

Leading Economic Index

One of the most interesting, and occasionally controversial, statistical series is the *leading economic index (LEI)*, a monthly series designed to tell us where the economy is headed. Essentially, the series is a predictive tool to tell us if, and approximately when, a recession might take place.

The LEI is released by The Conference Board at the beginning of every month and is calculated from a variety of government series released during the previous month.[17] It is one of our most closely watched indicators of future economic activity.

How Do We Interpret the Index?

In general, most observers focus on changes in the direction and duration of the index. For example, if the index declines for three consecutive months, the conventional wisdom is that the index has signaled that a recession is about to begin.

In the same way, three consecutive monthly increases are taken as a sign that the economy will prosper or continue to prosper. The most difficult case to interpret is one where the index goes up for several months and then down for several months—or moves in no particular pattern as it sometimes does when a turning point is near.

How Was the Index Developed?

Intuitively, the concept of a leading indicator is fairly easy to grasp. We start with the observation that the overall economy is made up of all types of economic activity. Next we ask, could it be that some activities take place or that some events occur in *advance* of

---

[17] The series was compiled by the U.S. Department of Commerce for almost 30 years, but was transferred to The Conference Board in December of 1995 as part of a budget-saving measure. The Conference Board is a private, not-for-profit, non-advocacy organization that publishes several other statistical series including the help-wanted advertising, consumer confidence, and business confidence indices.

changes in the overall economy? If so, perhaps we could focus on these activities and use them to predict how the entire economy might behave in the near future.

Back in the 1950s, the National Bureau of Economic Research thought this might be happening and so they compared thousands of statistical series to changes in real GNP (GDP is now used instead). One set of data examined was an index of stock prices, which, as it turned out, usually declined sharply just before a recession got underway.

Theoretically, the linkage between stock prices and overall spending makes sense. For example, if people feel poorer because of their losses in the market, they might decide to cut back on spending. If enough people feel poorer, their collective decision to spend less may actually affect economic growth.

By itself, however, a measure of stock price performance could not be used as the sole indicator of future economic activity because stock prices sometimes went down while the economy went up. Using the approach that there is safety in numbers, why not look for other statistical series to combine with stock prices?

It turned out that building permits for private housing also behaved somewhat like stock prices—with the total number of permits issued tending to decrease several months before the economy turned down. Again, this seems to make sense because a decline in building permits may well mean that a substantial amount of economic activity will either be delayed or not take place at all.

Eventually, the list was narrowed down to a handful and then combined to form a composite index. The resulting series usually changed direction some months *before* the economy did, hence the term "leading indicator." The index offered considerable promise, and so the Department of Commerce took over the task of collecting and publishing the data. Eventually, responsibility for compiling the series was transferred to The Conference Board, making it the first-ever privatization of an official U.S. government statistical series.

The list of component series in the index is presented in Table 3-1. The Department of Commerce revised the list in 1989, and it was revised again by The Conference Board in December 1996. The last

Table 3-1
Components of the Leading Economic Index

1. Average weekly hours of production workers in manufacturing
2. Average weekly initial claims for state unemployment insurance
3. Manufacturers' new orders for consumer goods and materials
4. Index of supplier deliveries—vendor performance diffusion index
5. Manufacturers' new orders, nondefense capital goods
6. New private housing authorized by local building permits
7. Stock prices, 500 common stocks
8. M2 money supply in 2000 dollars
9. Interest rate spread, 10-year Treasury bonds less federal funds rate
10. Index of consumer expectations (University of Michigan series)

Source: The Conference Board, April 2009

revision dropped two series in favor of the yield curve, which is a measure of the spread between long-term and short-term interest rates. This revision also made it an index of 10 (rather than 11) indicators, but the major concern is whether the performance of the index can be improved, not the number of individual components.

The Historical Record

Most of the controversy concerning the index focuses on whether or not three consecutive downturns actually forecast an economic slowdown. Figure 3-7 shows The Conference Board index where the shaded areas, as before, represent recessions so that we can compare the turning points of the index with real GDP contractions.

The figure shows that every recession since 1965 was preceded by a sharp drop in the leading economic index. The recession warnings given by the index averaged 8.4 months and ranged from as few as 3 to as many as 15 months.

Less important, but worth mentioning, is the ability of the index to predict when a recession is about to end. Figure 3-7 shows that the lead time ranged from 2 to 8 months, with 4.0 being the average. However, because it takes several months or more to recognize a turning point in the index, the economy is usually well out of the recession before the index signals the prediction.

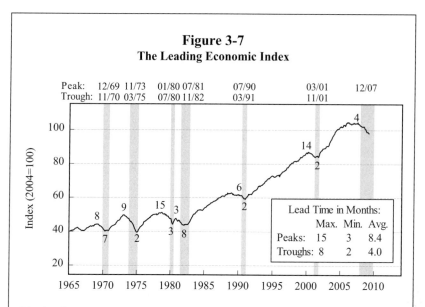

Figure 3-7
The Leading Economic Index

The leading economic index (LEI) appears to have predicted the latest recession starting in December 2007 by 4 months. This index is one of the most reliable and closely followed indicators of overall economic activity.

Did The Conference Board's Revisions Help?

Economists think so. In fact, the revisions resulted in three improvements. First, the size of the "false signal" in 1984 was muted. Second, the size of the 1989 downturn was more pronounced, giving a stronger warning of the impending recession. Third, the size of the false signal given in 1995 was reduced.

On the other hand, the historical data for the revised series still showed a false warning for mid-1966. Other revisions, such as the change to a newer base year, had no bearing on the turning points of the series. Overall, however, the LEI certainly performed well enough when it predicted the recession that began in December 2007, so it seems to be on track.

Has the Index Ever *Failed* to Predict a Recession?

You bet! The older BEA index had a number of successes, along with a few false alarms. One was in 1966 when the index turned down for nine consecutive months and the economy still continued to grow. However, heavy (and to some extent hidden) spending on the Vietnam War may have provided enough stimulus to avoid a recession.[18]

Another false prediction was in March 1984 when the index turned down for seven consecutive months. Again, however, massive federal deficit spending—to the tune of $200 billion annually in 1985 and 1986—seems to have provided enough stimulus to avoid a recession. Later, a series of declines in early 1995 presented another puzzling period for the leading index. At the time, it seemed that the index had peaked, but strong economic growth in 1996 suggests that 1995 was a relative, rather than an absolute, peak.

So, the short answer to our question is this: the leading economic index predicted every single recession since 1965—along with a few others that never occurred.

Are There Other Problems with the Index?

Frequent revisions of the monthly numbers are a major source of frustration. Whenever a new monthly composite index number is announced, revisions are also made to the six previous monthly numbers, primarily because the underlying individual component series are revised.

For example, suppose we have a period when the index has already turned down two months in a row. We anxiously await the next report, and it turns out to be another decline, but is coupled with an upward revision of an earlier (negative) number. This leaves us back where we started, with two *newer* consecutive months of decline—and our attention again riveted on the coming month's figures.

To make matters more interesting, some forecasters follow the individual component series that make up the composite index in hopes that they can forecast the change in the index that forecasts the change in the economy. As a result, the general direction of the

---

[18] Most economists exclude wartime periods because of distortion in the domestic statistics. The NBER, for example, compiles separate statistics on the length of peacetime expansions, contractions, and overall business cycles (see Table 2-2, page 26).

leading index is usually known and can be forecast before the official numbers are released.

Despite some of these issues, the leading economic index is a popular forecasting device. It is one of the main tools in the forecaster's tool kit, and one of the most-watched statistical series in the economy today.

Leading Economic Index

Indicator status:	Leading for recessions and recoveries
Compiled by:	The Conference Board
Frequency:	Monthly
Release date:	about 3-4 weeks after the closing of the survey month
Revisions:	Up to six previous months are revised with every new release
Published data:	*Business Cycle Indicators,* The Conference Board
Internet:	http://www.conference-board.org/
	http://www.EconSources.com

Chapter 4

INVESTMENT and CAPITAL EXPENDITURES

Private Nonresidential Fixed Investment

For the advance first-quarter estimate of 2009, total private investment expenditures, also known as *gross private domestic investment*, accounted for 11.2 percent of total GDP.[1] The majority of these private expenditures were for nonresidential purposes—structures, business equipment and software—and they make up a category called **gross private nonresidential fixed investment**. The nonresidential expenditure category accounted for only 9.5 percent of total GDP in that quarter, but they are extremely important.

On a percentage basis, neither measure may seem to be a very big portion of total output, so why are economists so interested in this component of GDP? The answer is rooted in the long search for stable and predictable economic relationships.

The Search for Stable Relationships

When Keynes wrote his magnificent *General Theory of Employment, Interest, and Money* during the Great Depression of the 1930s, he offered a bold and radical explanation of how the economy functioned.[2] His approach was based on a conceptual framework that broke the economy down into sectors and then described, in considerable detail, the spending behavior of each.

---

[1] From Table 2-3 on page 29.

[2] John Maynard Keynes, *The General Theory of Employment, Interest, and Money*, Harcourt, Brace & Co., New York, 1936.

Keynes argued that spending by consumers, more commonly called spending by the consumer sector, was relatively stable. This was important because if it could be shown that the greater part of total economic activity behaved in a relatively stable and predictable manner, then the instability of the total economy must be due to other—and smaller—components.

Despite the fact that there were no existing GDP statistics that could be used to verify his convictions, Keynes' description of spending by each sector—consumer, business, government, and the international or foreign sector—was so detailed that academicians started collecting data to test his theories. In the end, research largely confirmed the propositions put forth in the *General Theory*. Before long, the data grew into the NIPA accounts that feature the GDP, GNP, NNP, and other measures of aggregate economic performance that we use today.[3] These accounts, along with the organization of Tables 2-3, 4-1, and numerous other tables and figures used throughout this book, are directly influenced by Keynes' work.

Table 4-1 illustrates the spending stability by four main sectors of the economy. The table follows the format of Table 2-3, only this time the focus is on the quarterly percentage changes of GDP components over time. The first column shows the relative spending for each of the various categories in the first quarter of 2009; with the consumer sector accounting for 70.7 percent of total expenditures, the government sector accounting for 20.4 percent, the businesses sector accounting for 11.2 percent, and the foreign sector with −2.4 percent. Columns 2 and 3 show the maximum and minimum percentage changes for each category, and the mean percentage change is shown in the fourth column. The coefficient of variation, a measure of relative dispersion, appears in the last column.[4]

Even the most casual inspection of the table reveals the stability of the consumer sector and the relative instability of the

---

[3] Simon Kuznets, the second American to win the Nobel Prize in economics, was already working on a set of national income accounts when Keynes was working on *The General Theory*. His data were used to test some of the theories put forth by Keynes.

[4] The coefficient of variation (CV) is the standard deviation divided by the mean—a measure that allows us to compare the variability of two series with different means. To illustrate, the CV of 0.8 for personal consumption expenditures tells us that quarterly percentage changes for this sector are one of the most stable in the table. A CV of 3.8 for gross private domestic investment means that quarterly percentage changes in this series are roughly 5 times (or 3.8/.8) more volatile than personal consumption expenditures.

Table 4-1
Quarterly Percentage Changes in Real GDP Components, 1965-2009-I

	% of GDP in 2009-I	Maximum Change	Minimum Change	Mean Change	CV
Gross domestic product	*100.0*	*16.7%*	*-7.8%*	*3.1%*	*1.1*
*Personal consumption expenditures**	*70.7*	*11.7%*	*-8.6%*	*3.4%*	*0.8*
Durable goods	6.8	53.2%	-37.8%	6.0%	2.2
Nondurable goods	20.0	14.6%	-9.4%	2.6%	1.1
Services	43.9	8.0%	2.4%	3.5%	0.5
Gross private domestic investment†	*11.2*	*63.2%*	*-53.7%*	*4.7%*	*3.8*
Fixed investment	12.2	32.4%	-37.9%	3.8%	2.6
Nonresidential	9.5	38.3%	-37.9%	4.8%	2.1
Residential	2.7	87.6%	-55.9%	2.8%	7.1
Change in private inventories	-1.0	--	--	--	--
Net exports of goods and services‡	*-2.4*	--	--	--	--
Exports	10.9	124.5%	-40.0%	6.8%	2.5
Import	13.3	105.4%	-34.4%	7.0%	2.3
Govt. purchases of goods, services§	*20.4*	*18.1%*	*-8.0%*	*2.2%*	*1.9*
Federal	7.8	30.4%	-19.9%	1.8%	4.3
State and local	12.6	12.4%	-7.5%	2.6%	1.3

*Consumer sector   †Business sector   §Government sector   ‡Foreign Sector

investment sector, or gross private domestic investment, that was predicted by Keynes.[5] This instability should be enough to make it worthy of study—but there's more. Investment sector expenditures, Keynes argued, have a way of causing *additional* expenditures through the multiplier principle.[6]

The multiplier is defined as the change in overall spending caused by a change in investment spending—and the multiplier works in *both* directions. On one hand, a reduction of investment spending would translate into an even larger reduction in overall spending, which Keynes felt was at least partially responsible for the Great Depression of the 1930s. On the other hand, "pump priming" in the

---

[5] The BEA did not show the quarterly percentage changes for either the change in private inventories or the net export of goods and services entries in their historical Table 1.1.1, so we were not able to compute CVs for either. However, the first entry is relatively small as a percentage of GDP, and the second entry—the net foreign sector—was much smaller and less significant when Keynes published the *General Theory* in 1936.

[6] The President's Council of Economic Advisors has estimated that the multiplier for the United States economy is about 2. This means that $1 billion of investment spending will ultimately generate about $2 billion of total output.

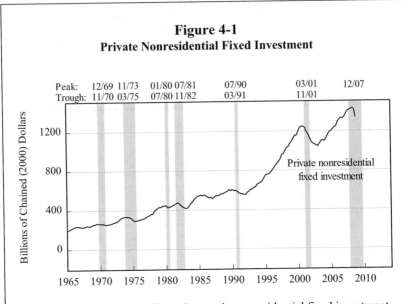

Figure 4-1
Private Nonresidential Fixed Investment

Because of the multiplier effect, changes in nonresidential fixed investment expenditures have a magnified impact on real GDP. This series tracks the 9.5 percent of total GDP shown in Table 4-1.

form of additional government spending would have the opposite impact—that of causing even more overall spending in hopes that it would put the economy back on track to recovery and growth.

The nonresidential fixed investment series plotted in Figure 4-1 gives us a visual feel for the relative instability of business sector spending—instability that is further magnified by the presence of the multiplier. This instability is especially evident when the figure is compared to consumer spending such as that shown in Figure 6-1 on page 97.

Declines in fixed investment normally accompany a recession. Sometimes, as in mid-2000, the decline preceded the recession by several months. At other times, as in the second quarter of 2008, the decline started several months after the recession began. In almost every case, however, investment did not recover until well after the recession ended. Clearly expenditures by this sector warrant close attention if we are concerned about the stability of GDP.

Looking Back—But Not Forward

At one time, the government even kept a series on planned or new plant and equipment expenditures. Eventually, however, the level of planned plant and equipment expenditures did not track well with the actual, and so it was dropped after the second quarter of 1994 in favor of a new semiannual series based on an Annual Capital Expenditures Survey (ACES).[7]

Unfortunately, these plans were then dropped for budgetary reasons even before any data were ever published. And so, despite the obvious importance of investment sector spending, and despite numerous monthly series that track specific investment sector categories, the federal government currently has no forward-looking series regarding planned capital expenditures.

The reason we watch the private nonresidential investment series is that it helps explain some of the observed variations in real GDP. The downside is that it, like many of the other NIPA components, is a quarterly report that does a better job of telling us where we are, rather than where we are headed.

Private Nonresidential Fixed Investment

Indicator status:	Mostly coincident for recessions; lagging for recoveries
Compiled by:	Bureau of Economic Analysis
Frequency:	Quarterly
Release date:	End of the month with GDP revisions
Revisions:	Advance, revised, and final revisions along with GDP revisions
Published data:	*Economic Indicators*, Council of Economic Advisors *Survey of Current Business*, U.S. Department of Commerce
Internet:	http://www.bea.doc.gov http://www.EconSources.com

---

[7] At the beginning of the year, firms would report their plans for first-quarter spending. If these plans were delayed, some respondents would simply push the planned expenditures ahead to the next quarter. When the last quarter arrived, however, there was a tendency for firms to simply cancel the delayed expenditures altogether, thus causing distortions in the quarterly figures. To make matters worse, benchmark revisions that were normally done every 5 years or so to assure the validity of the sample were not conducted after 1982. As a result, the series became less and less reliable with respect to the level of capital expenditures, although there was less concern with the timing of the turning points.

Building Permits and Housing Starts

According to Table 4-1 on page 61, residential construction amounted to 2.7 percent of total GDP in the first quarter of 2009. This may not seem like a relatively large part of overall economic activity, especially given the state of the depressed housing market in 2009-I, but the problem is that the multiplier amplifies this negative change on the rest of the economy. Several series are often used to track housing activity, but two that receive the most attention will be discussed here: the number of new building permits issued, and statistics on the number of new homes started.[8]

The first series is formally known as *new private housing units authorized by local building permits*—which explains the more common and considerably shorter title. The building permits series is also the only housing series included in the composite *index of leading indicators* although other series are available.[9] The second measure discussed here is *new private housing units started* series. This differs from new building permits in that it represents actual homebuilding activity, not just the *intention* to build.[10] Both series are released mid-month following the reference month.

Do Building Permits Predict Future Economic Activity?

On one level, the relationship between new building permits issued and overall economic activity may seem tenuous. After all, a

---

[8] Two others are *gross private residential fixed investment* in constant dollars and the Department of Housing and Urban Development's (HUD) series on the sales of new homes. The former tracks the housing component of the NIPA accounts and is reported quarterly. The latter reports total dollar sales rather than thousands of units, as is the case of housing starts.

[9] The preliminary release, on a seasonally adjusted annual basis, is available on the twelfth workday of every month and is the one reported in the press. The final figures for the series are available on the eighteenth workday and are the ones included in the *index of leading indicators*.

[10] Housing starts and building permits do not include mobile home units.

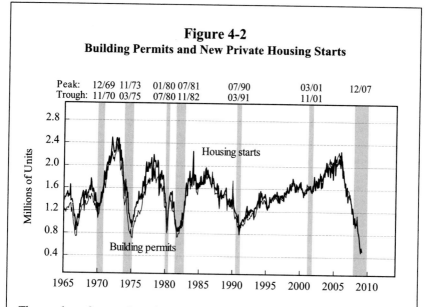

Figure 4-2
Building Permits and New Private Housing Starts

The number of new private housing (building) permits and new private housing units started both function as leading indicators for recessions and recoveries. The main problem with both series is the relative size of the month-to-month variations which can obscure the underlying trend.

building permit represents the intention to spend rather than an actual commitment to spend. The intent to build may even be adversely affected by changes in interest rates after the permit is issued. As a result, the amount of time between issuance of the permit and the start of the new residence may vary significantly.

A building permit is also relatively inexpensive to obtain and is sometimes acquired partially for precautionary reasons—for example, "in case" the opportunity to build is right. Last but not least, some regions of the country do not require building permits, so the number of starts can exceed the number of permits. In short, there are several reasons why the number of building permits issued might not work very well as an economic indicator.

The Historical Record

But, work well they do. As can be seen in Figure 4-2, in most cases the new private building permits series tends to increase sharply during the early years of an economic expansion and then decline sharply some months or years before the recession begins. Then, while the economy is in recession, the index tends to shoot up dramatically, foretelling the impending recovery.

A major problem, clearly evident in Figure 4-2, is the volatility of the series. Monthly double-digit changes are not infrequent, and a large change in one direction is often followed by a sharp reversal the very next month. To illustrate, in February 2008 building permits went up by 6.2% only to be followed by a 9.0% drop the next month.

Some of the volatility is due to the nature of the series, but some is also due to sampling variability. For example, the Census Bureau uses a mail survey to collect building permit data from local building permit officials. When requested reports are not received, missing values are simply estimated.

What About Housing Starts?

This series is similar to building permits in that it is expressed in terms of thousands of private houses started annually. It also exhibits a high degree of volatility. To illustrate, housing starts increased by 17.2 percent in February 2009 and then declined by 10.8 percent in March.

Weather is often the cause of such changes. Since permits are relatively inexpensive and easy to obtain, a builder may have a backlog of building permits and may be waiting for favorable weather to begin construction. Changing interest rates are another factor, especially when the Fed actively raises or lowers interest rates to control inflation or stimulate the economy.

Is One Preferable to the Other?

The good news is that both series function reasonably well as leading indicators for both peaks and troughs in overall economic activity. As far as the peaks are concerned, Figure 4-2 clearly shows severe and protracted drops in both series just before the recessionary periods.

The bad news is that both series are so volatile that monthly revisions of the initial preliminary estimates often include changes in the *direction* of movement as well as magnitude. As a result, the Census Bureau claims that "it may take 3 months to establish an underlying trend for building permit authorizations, 4 months for total starts, and 5 months for total completions."[11]

The main problem with building permits and housing starts is one of interpretation as the focus often seems to be on the size of the preliminary monthly change rather than on the underlying trend. It just takes a few months for the data to be revised and the trend established, so we have to be patient and not put too much emphasis on the most recent monthly report.

Building Permits and Housing Starts

Indicator status:	Both series: leading for recessions and recoveries
Compiled by:	Census Bureau
Frequency:	Monthly
Release date:	Preliminary (both series): twelfth workday of the month
	Final (both series): eighteenth workday of the month
Revisions:	Building permits: previous two months revised monthly; annual revision every April
	Housing starts: previous two months revised monthly; annual revision every January
Published data:	*New Residential Construction*, Census Bureau, U.S. Department of Commerce
	Economic Indicators, Council of Economic Advisors
Internet:	http://www.census.gov/const/www/newresconstindex.html
	http://www.EconSources.com

---

[11] U.S. Census Bureau News Joint Release, *New Residential Construction in March 2009*, April 16, 2009.

Business Inventories

Historically, inventories have played an important role in the literature on recessions and expansions.[12] In general, high levels of inventories have been singled out as contributing to the cause of recessions, while low inventories are sometimes thought to be a sign that business activity is about to pick up. To see how this might come about, let's take a simplistic look at the process.

How Do Inventory Levels Affect Economic Activity?

First, it helps to think of inventories as being a buffer between production and sales. Suppose, for example, that consumers suddenly and unexpectedly cut back on their spending. The result is likely to be levels of unsold business inventories at stores and warehouses. If businesses react by reducing orders from suppliers, or by closing plants, workers will either work shorter hours or lose their jobs.

This, in turn, reduces the amount of income workers have to spend, which may cause inventory levels to again *increase*, rather than decrease, as businesses had planned. If the cycle repeats itself, production will again fall, unemployment will rise, and consumer spending will drop, all of which may put the economy firmly on the path to recession.

Eventually, businesses may succeed in reducing production to the point where inventories are too low. If they overshoot their mark, or if consumer spending increases even slightly, inventory shortages may develop. Businesses will then need to hire more instead of fewer workers. This increases employment and consumer spending, causing inventories to go down again rather than up. As long as businesses

---

[12] W.S. Jevons, Wesley Mitchell, and John Maynard Keynes were but a few of the many economists to incorporate the role of inventories into their view of the causes and explanations of economic fluctuations. In the late 1940s, Moses Abramovitz's classic work, *The Role of Inventories in Business Cycles*, was published by the National Bureau of Economic Research and did much to influence the way inventory statistics are compiled and reported today.

continue to try to replenish inventories, the process of playing catch-up helps pull the economy out of recession and puts it on the path to recovery.

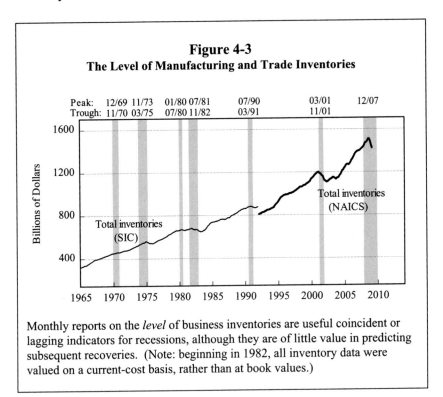

Figure 4-3
The Level of Manufacturing and Trade Inventories

Monthly reports on the *level* of business inventories are useful coincident or lagging indicators for recessions, although they are of little value in predicting subsequent recoveries. (Note: beginning in 1982, all inventory data were valued on a current-cost basis, rather than at book values.)

Does It Really Work Like That?

As can be seen in Figure 4-3, the level of inventories tends to turn down as, or shortly after, the recession begins, which makes it a coincident or a lagging indicator for recessions. In fact, any series that reports on the *level* of inventories is usually more of a lagging indicator than a coincident one.

Of course there is always more than one way to look at a series, so let's try again. This time, in Figure 4-4, we will look at the *change* in the level of inventories rather than at the level itself.

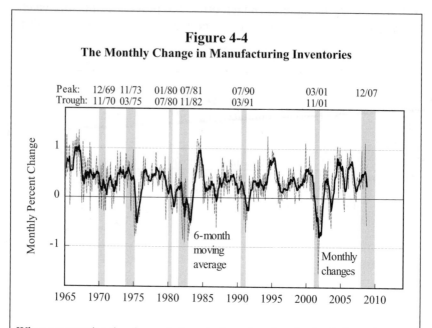

Figure 4-4
The Monthly Change in Manufacturing Inventories

Peak: 12/69 11/73   01/80 07/81   07/90   03/01   12/07
Trough: 11/70 03/75   07/80 11/82   03/91   11/01

When we examine the *change* in inventories rather than the *level*, the series behaves more like a leading indicator. Because month-to-month fluctuations are so wide, a 6-month moving average can be used to smooth the series. Note that the series does not have to predict every single recession and expansion in order to be classified as a leading indicator—it just has to work most of the time.

According to this series, the monthly percentage change in the level of inventories looks more like a leading indicator for recessions—with the series usually reaching a peak well before GDP turns down. The leading tendencies are more evident when a moving average is used to reduce the volatility, so the series gives us yet another way to look at inventories as an economic indicator.

So Why Bother with Inventory Levels?

Because others do! In fact, many financial writers insist on reporting the level of business inventories (or a given subset) even though it is not helpful as an indicator of future economic activity. In addition, such reports often cite the series in current (inflation biased), not constant, dollars. When this happens, the monthly series is more likely to just go up, depending on the severity of the underlying inflation. [13]

What Should We Remember About Inventory Statistics?

First, any series that reports changes in the level of inventories tends to act as a coincident or lagging indicator. Second, if we look at changes in the level of inventories, the data now behave more as leading indicators. Monthly percentage changes are highly variable, however, and so moving averages are often used to smooth the data. Third, as difficult as inventories, or changes in inventories, are to track, they are nevertheless important because they are one of the most volatile of our GDP components.

Business Inventories

Indicator status:	Inventory levels are coincident or lagging indicators for recessions; *changes* in the level are leading indicators for recessions, coincident for recoveries
Compiled by:	Bureau of Economic Analysis
Frequency:	Monthly
Release date:	Six weeks after the close of the reference month
Revisions:	3 times every quarter as GDP is revised; annual revision in July for the previous 3 years
Published data:	*Economic Indicators*, Council of Economic Advisors *Manufacturing and Trade Inventories and Sales*, and *Survey of Current Business*, U.S. Department of Commerce
Internet:	http://www.census.gov/mtis/www/current.html http://www.EconSources.com

---

[13] The first release of numbers from any agency in the Department of Commerce is usually on a current-dollar basis. This happens because the price index series used to convert current dollars to chain-weighted (or real) dollars is not immediately available.

Inventory/Sales Ratio

Inventories may be a relatively small part of the overall economic picture, but their volatility is such that they attract more than their fair share of attention.[14] As a result, yet another way to examine the role of inventories is to combine them with sales in the form of a ratio. The Census Bureau compiles several ratios of inventories to sales, but the most comprehensive is the monthly **total business inventories/sales ratio** that appears approximately six weeks following the close of the reference month.

Advantages of Ratios

Among the many advantages of ratios, two stand out. First, ratios can be constructed from other statistical series without actually having to collect new data. Second, ratios allow us to observe the interaction between two related series such as inventories and sales.

To illustrate, and in the absence of other information, it would be reasonable to assume that rising inventory levels would be a likely consequence of declining sales. Either change by itself would be a matter of concern, but a ratio of the two—with the numerator getting larger and the denominator getting smaller—would show even more movement. In this case, a simple ratio of inventories to sales might be a good indicator that one or both of the series is changing.

Leading Indicator Status

The proof of the pudding, it is often said, "is in the eating"—or in Figure 4-5 to be more exact. Specifically, the inventory/sales ratio in the figure is far more stable than monthly percentage changes in inventory levels that are shown in Figure 4-4.

---

[14] The monthly percentage changes in private inventories are typically so high that the BEA chose not to report them in their historical tables (see the footnote on page 61). However, change they do, and so they contribute significantly to the relative instability of the business sector.

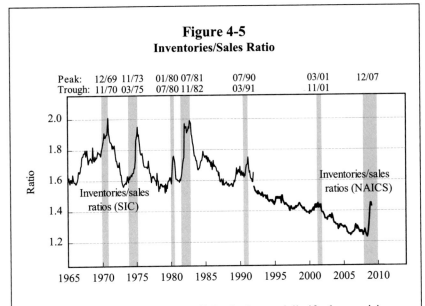

Figure 4-5
Inventories/Sales Ratio

Rising inventory levels may not be all that bad, especially if sales are rising even faster. As a result, the inventory/sales ratio is useful because it shows the relationship between two related series. The ratio has considerable value as a leading indicator of future economic downturns.

Overall, the ratio has behaved well as a leading indicator for recessions—turning up well before the recession arrives. Several changes have been made that affect the data from the early 1990s to the present, but the principle is the same and the variability of the series has been significantly reduced as evidenced in Figure 4-5.

Inventories/Sales Ratio	
Indicator status:	Leading economic indicator for recessions
Compiled by:	Census Bureau
Frequency:	Monthly
Release date:	Mid-month following the reference month
Revisions:	Approximately 10 days after the initial mid-month release
Published data:	*Manufacturing and Trade Inventories and Sales*
	U.S. Department of Commerce
	Economic Indicators, Council of Economic Advisors
Internet:	http://www.census.gov/mtis/www/current.html
	http://www.EconSources.com

Durable Goods Orders

Durable goods, goods that last at least three years under normal use, constitute a significant part of overall economy. The 6.8 percent of GDP shown in Table 4-1 is the spending by the consumer sector only—and would be about twice that size if we included the spending on durables by the business and nondefense government sectors.

The series on durable goods is called ***manufacturers' new orders, durable goods industries*** and is a measure of the durable goods intended for the business sector. This statistic, representing about 6 percent of total GDP, is compiled monthly from survey data gathered from approximately 4,300 reporting units. Advanced data are then released 3-4 weeks after the close of the reference month.

How Do Durable Goods *Orders* Differ from *Production*?

There are several important differences. First, there is the difference in coverage mentioned above, with the series on durable goods orders representing a much smaller portion of GDP. Second, the Federal Reserve System collects data on the production of all durable goods, whereas the Census Bureau, which is part of the Department of Commerce, collects the data on durable goods orders.

Third, data on durable goods orders are reported in billions of dollars rather than in the form of an index. Historical data are available in terms of real (chained) dollars, although the Census Bureau favors reports in the form of month-to-month percentage changes—thereby avoiding the issue of choosing between current or constant dollar amounts. The historical measure for new orders of durable goods is shown in Figure 4-6.

Just How Useful Is the Series?

Overall, the series gives an uneven performance as a leading indicator because it is so volatile from one month to the next. In fact, the series turns down about as often as it turns up, even though there

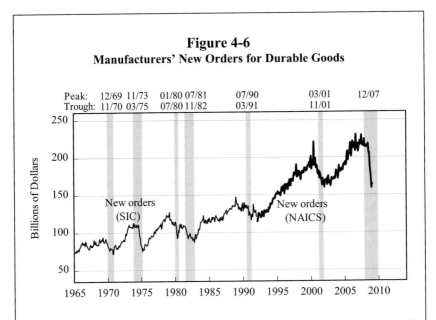

Figure 4-6
Manufacturers' New Orders for Durable Goods

New orders for durable goods may have leading indicator status, but the monthly numbers are so volatile that it is sometimes difficult to identify relative peaks and troughs. For the NAICS series shown in this figure, there were 95 monthly declines and 111 monthly increases.

are many more expansion years than recessionary ones. Even during the 2008 recession year, durable goods orders changed signs, or directions, six different times.

In addition to these frequent changes of direction, some of the monthly changes can be quite dramatic. For example, in September 2006, new orders for durable goods rose 10.3 percent, only to decrease by 8.3 percent the very next month. Whenever a statistical series exhibits this much volatility, it is difficult to infer much from any one monthly change. It is more useful when looked at over a longer period of time, and it may be better to use a moving average to smooth out the short-term changes, although this is currently not done.

Unfortunately, a large change in any statistical series can capture the attention of the press, and too much is often made of it. This is especially true when most of the other economic indicators are giving mixed signals—a combination of events that encourages people to look for more significance in a series than is really warranted.

Overall, the durable goods orders series has historically performed as a leading indicator. It tends to peak before the economy peaks and to bottom out before the economy bottoms out. However, the variability of the lead times, along with the number and size of the monthly changes, means that this indicator should be interpreted with caution.

Durable Goods Orders	
Indicator status:	Leading economic indicator for recessions and recoveries
Compiled by:	Census Bureau
Frequency:	Monthly
Release date:	Advance report about 18 working days after the end of the reference month
Revisions:	Regular report about 23 working days after end of month; revisions in the spring, benchmarks every 5 years
Published data:	*Economic Indicators*, Council of Economic Advisors
Internet:	http://www.census.gov/m3 http://www.EconSources.com

Chapter 5

EMPLOYMENT and UNEMPLOYMENT

Total Employment

Numbers on employment and earnings are important to all of us. At a personal level, being employed means that we can take home a paycheck, and that's something that is near and dear to everyone. At the macroeconomic level, changes in the total number of people employed tell us a lot about the state of the economy. Even the National Bureau of Economic Research (NBER) uses the total employment situation to help establish the beginning and ending dates of a recession.[1]

While several statistical series would allow us to follow employment trends, one of our favorites is the **total nonfarm payroll employment** series that is released monthly by the Bureau of Labor Statistics.

Collecting Employment Statistics

Every month, state agencies use a national survey provided by the Bureau of Labor Statistics to collect data on employment, hours and earnings from approximately 390,000 business establishments. The survey covers the workweek containing the 12th of the month, and the businesses covered by the survey employ approximately 40 percent of the nonfarm population. This effort provides the data for the *Current Employment Statistics* (CES) survey that is the source of nonfarm payroll estimates for total employment, average weekly hours worked, and average hourly earnings.

---

[1] The NBER business cycle dating procedure is discussed in more detail on pages 24-27.

Because there are so many parties involved in the collection of the data, it often takes several months to get a complete picture of developments in any particular month. For example, three Fridays after the close of the week containing the 12th, a preliminary report is issued based on approximately 60 percent of the surveys that will ultimately be received. About a month after that, when approximately 80 percent of the surveys have been collected, a second preliminary estimate is prepared. A "final" estimate is then released in the third month when more than 90 percent of the surveys are processed.

What Does It Take To Be Employed?

Not much. Specifically, a person is classified as being employed if, during the reference week, he or she did any work at all as a paid employee; worked in their own business or profession for pay; or worked without pay at least 15 hours in a family business. This means that a person who worked only one hour for pay during the survey week would be considered employed.[2]

In addition, the survey does not distinguish between full- and part-time workers, and even temporary or occasional workers are included if they happen to be on the job when the survey is taken. This means that a worker who works two or three jobs could conceivably be counted multiple times during the survey week.

The Historical Record

Figure 5-1 shows the growth of total nonfarm employment since 1965. As you can see in the figure, total employment turns down at the beginning of a recession and then starts to recover at about the time, or shortly after, the recession ends. However, the figure also shows that it took even longer—from 12-18 months—for employment to recover following the 1990-91 and 2001 recessions.

For the period shown in Figure 5-1, the total employment decline was especially intense during the recent 2008-09 recession.

---

[2] See the "New Jobs Created" statistic on page 80 for more on this. Workers who have a job but are out on strike and therefore receive no pay, and workers who are on unpaid sick leave and do not receive pay during the survey week, are not counted as being employed. However, workers on paid vacation, or paid sick leave, are counted as being employed because they collect some pay for all or some of the workweek.

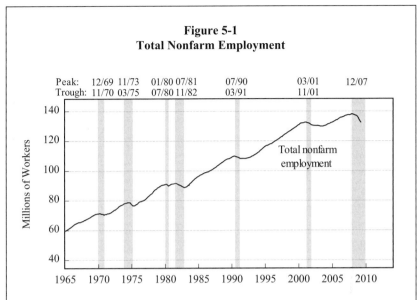

Figure 5-1
Total Nonfarm Employment

Total employment dropped by almost 4.2 percent between December 2007 and April 2009—a painful and historically steep drop. Because employment does not recover until after the end of a recession, it has the characteristics of a lagging economic indicator for recoveries.

To illustrate, the 2.7 million job losses that occurred in the 30 months that followed the March 2001 peak were more than matched in the first 12 months that followed the beginning of the December 2007 downturn. The bottom line is that job losses can occur relatively suddenly, and too often they are too slow to come back.

Total Nonfarm Employment	
Indicator status:	Coincident for recessions, lagging for recoveries
Compiled by:	Bureau of Labor Statistics
Frequency:	Monthly
Release date:	First Friday of the following month
Revisions:	Preliminary estimate revised the next two months; annual benchmark revisions every June
Published data:	*Economic Indicators,* Council of Economic Advisors
	The Employment Situation, Bureau of Labor Statistics
Internet:	http://www.bls.gov
	http://www.EconSources.com

New Jobs Created

One of the most frequently cited "statistics" in the press is called *new jobs created*—but it is not really a statistic in the traditional sense of the word. Instead, it is a monthly number released by the Bureau of Labor Statistics (BLS) and its prominence seems to be due to the attention paid to it by the press and politicians alike. For example, how many times have we heard that X number of jobs were lost/gained in a given month, or how many times have we heard a politician say that he or she will create X million jobs if elected?

The Monthly "New Jobs Created" Number

On the first Friday of every month the BLS reports on the latest employment situation in its *Employment Situation Summary*. This report, part of which is reproduced in Table 5-1, is the source of the new jobs created/lost number and it is the source of the monthly unemployment rate discussed in the next section as well.

For example, if we take a look at the table (modified to fit the page), we can see that there were 13,161,000 people unemployed in a civilian labor force of 154,048,000. If we then divide the number of unemployed persons by the labor force, we get the 8.5 percent unemployment rate for all workers shown in the table. The change in total nonfarm employment of -663 in the middle of the table is the difference between the two preliminary employment numbers for February and March and is interpreted to mean that 663,000 jobs have been "lost"—or "created" if the number had been positive.

Monthly BLS Employment Numbers

Table 5-1 also shows that the data come from two different sources. The first is the "Household Data" from the *Current Population Survey* (*CPS*) done by the Census Bureau; the second is "Establishment Data" from the BLS's *Current Employment Statistics* (*CES*) survey—and it turns out that the data seldom matches.

Table 5-1

Major indicators of labor market activity, seasonally adjusted
(Numbers in thousands)

Category	Quarterly averages		Monthly data			Feb.-Mar. change
	IV 2008	I 2009	Jan. 2009	Feb. 2009	Mar. 2009	
HOUSEHOLD DATA			Labor force status			
Civilian labor force	154,648	153,993	153,716	154,214	**154,048**	-166
Employment	144,046	141,578	142,099	141,748	140,887	-861
Unemployment	10,602	12,415	11,616	12,467	**13,161**	694
Not in labor force	80,177	80,920	81,023	80,699	81,038	339
			Unemployment rates			
All workers	6.9	8.1	7.6	8.1	**8.5**	0.4
Teenagers	20.7	21.3	20.8	21.6	21.7	.1
White	6.3	7.4	6.9	7.3	7.9	.6
Black or African/Amer..	11.5	13.1	12.6	13.4	13.3	-.1
Hispanic or Latino	8.9	10.7	9.7	10.9	11.4	.5
ESTABLISHMENT DATA			Employment			
Nonfarm employment.......	135,727	p133,678	134,333	p133,682	p133,019	**p-663**
Goods-producing (1)....	20,803	p19,835	20,127	p19,842	p19,537	p-305
Service-providing (1)..	114,924	p113,843	114,206	p113,840	p113,482	p-358
Retail trade (2)...	15,127	p14,942	14,992	p14,941	p14,893	p-48
Professional and business services .	17,485	p17,042	17,205	p17,027	p16,894	p-133
Education and health services	19,035	p19,136	19,119	p19,141	p19,149	p8
Leisure and hospitality	13,348	p13,236	13,268	p13,240	p13,200	p-40
Government	22,538	p22,540	22,540	p22,543	p22,538	p-5
			Hours of work (3)			
Total private	33.4	p33.3	33.3	p33.3	p33.2	p-0.1
			Earnings (3)			
Average hourly earnings, total private	$18.34	p$18.47	$18.43	p$18.47	p$18.50	p$0.03
Average weekly earnings, total private	612.55	p614.32	613.72	p615.05	p614.20	p-.85

Source: Table A, Monthly *Employment Situation Summary*, Bureau of Labor Statistics, March 2009.

To illustrate, suppose you worked 20 hours a week at a department store and 17 hours a week at McBurger's. The establishment survey would reveal two jobs, but the household survey would find only one person employed. To reconcile the difference, the BLS simply combines the two and records one person as being employed 37 hours at the establishment, or business, where the most hours are worked.

Because part-time jobs have become so prevalent in our economy, total employment as measured by the CES survey of business establishments usually grows faster than employment measured by the household survey. After all, if you were to lose your full-time job and then replace it with three part-time ones, the "new jobs created" series would go up by two jobs. It is this growth in the establishment survey that is usually cited as the source of the new jobs created or lost "statistic."

The Historical Record

Figure 5-2 shows what this series would look like if we plotted the monthly data from 1965 until the present.[3] As you can see, the monthly changes in total nonfarm employment are highly variable. Also, the monthly changes plotted in the figure are themselves the differences between two preliminary figures, so the reliability is even more suspect.

So Why the Popularity?

We don't know for sure, but we'd venture to guess that the so-called new jobs created/lost number is popular for several reasons.

First, the title is catchy and so it is easy for the popular press to write about tens of thousands of jobs coming or going away. Second, the monthly number is easily found in the monthly *Employment Situation Summary*, even if it is based on preliminary data that have not been smoothed. Third, the number seems to almost have a life of

---

[3] Monthly numbers for this series are not directly available, although they can be derived from the total nonfarm employment series that was used to generate Figure 5-1 on page 79. All we had to do was compute the differences between all of the monthly numbers and then plot the results in Figure 5-2.

Figure 5-2
"New Jobs Created" – The Monthly *Changes* in Total Employment

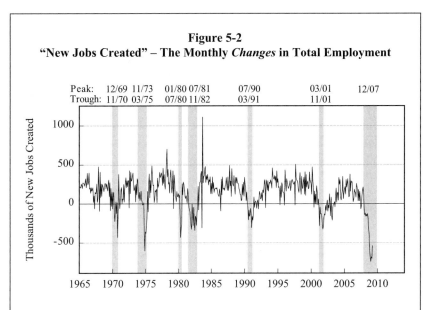

The New Jobs Created "statistic" is the monthly change in the total nonfarm employment series. It is widely reported in the press, and it is often cited by politicians, but it is not a historical series in the usual sense of the term.

its own in political circles where politicians seem to think that their personal philosophies and promised actions will actually add more jobs to the American economy than will the actions of the other candidates. As a result, we often hear about all of the new jobs that will be created when we enter a new election cycle.

Despite these qualifications, we also acknowledge that the numbers can often be interesting, even if they aren't as useful as others seem to think they are. After all, if the numbers are big enough, or if they consistently go in one direction or the other, they can provide useful information about the economy's health, or lack thereof.

Unemployment Rate

Unemployment numbers, specifically those in the ***civilian unemployment rate***, or simply the ***unemployment rate***, are among the most widely watched of all economic statistics. The rate can move as much as one or two percentage points in a short time, but it has remained within a much smaller range since the Great Depression of the 1930s when it peaked at nearly 25 percent.

How Are the Data Collected?

Unemployment data are collected monthly by the Census Bureau for the Bureau of Labor Statistics (BLS) using a survey covering about 60,000 households in approximately 2,000 counties and independent cities, with coverage in all 50 states and the District of Columbia. The survey is called the Current Population Survey (CPS), and it is the source of most labor market data, including earnings differentials among worker groups, labor force participation rates, and demographic characteristics of workers.

For consistency, the CPS is conducted in the week containing the 19th day of the month, with most questions relating to the week of the 12th day of the month. The BLS then compiles the data and usually issues labor force information on the first Friday of the following month. Sample survey questions are shown in Figure 5-3.[4]

---

[4] From 1967 to 1993, the CPS questionnaire remained essentially unchanged. During that time, however, a number of changes in the economy such as the growth of service jobs, the decline of factory jobs, the growing role of women, and the proliferation of alternative work schedules, took place. As a result, a computer-automated questionnaire with slightly revised questions was introduced in 1994 in an effort to achieve more accurate results. Under the old format, interviewers were equipped with a written list of questions, and the next question would be selected based on the answer to the previous question. Under the revised format, each of the 1,500 Census Bureau interviewers uses a portable computer that automatically selects the next question for them. The revised questions, shown in Figure 5-3, and the automated system generate more reliable results, but they also resulted in unemployment numbers that are about one-half a percentage higher than before. Consequently, the numbers we obtain today are not directly comparable to the ones obtained prior to 1994.

Figure 5-3
Current Population Survey – Selected Employment and Unemployment Questions

1. Does anyone in this household have a business or a farm?

2. LAST WEEK, did you do ANY work for (either) pay (or profit)?

   If 1 is "yes" and 2 is "no," ask 3.

3. LAST WEEK, did you do any unpaid work in the family business or farm?

   If 2 and 3 are both "no," ask 4.

4. LAST WEEK (in addition to the business), did you have a job, either full- or part-time? Include any job from which you were temporarily absent.

   If 4 is "no," ask 5.

5. LAST WEEK, were you on layoff from a job?

   If 5 is "yes," ask 6. If 5 is "no," ask 8.

6. Has your employer given you a date to return to work?

   If "no," ask 7.

7. Have you been given any indication that you will be recalled to work within the next 6 months?

   If "no," ask 8.

8. Have you been doing anything to find work during the last 4 weeks?

   If "yes," ask 9.

9. What are all of the things you have done to find work during the last 4 weeks?

Individuals are classified as **employed** if they say "yes" to questions 2, 3 (and worked 15 hours or more in the reference week or received profits from the business/farm), or 4.

Individuals available to work are classified as **unemployed** if they say "yes" to 5 and either 6 or 7, or if they say "yes" to 8 and provide a job search method that could have brought them into contact with a potential employer in 9.

Source: The questions above are from *Briefing Materials on the Redesigned Current Population Survey*, by the Bureau of Labor Statistics staff, February 4, 1994.

The Civilian Labor Force

One of the measures that comes out of the CPS is what economists call the *civilian labor force,* which consists of all civilians 16 years or older who are not confined to an institution and are not on active duty in the armed forces. Since members of the armed forces are always considered to be employed, and since members of the armed forces could make up a small—under two percent—but significant part of the labor force, the unemployment rate would go down if we included several million more people who all had jobs.

The part of the definition concerning the noninstitutional population is also intended to exclude those confined to a mental hospital or prison. After all, they can hardly be expected to be able to go out and seek, let alone hold, a job. Finally, the age limitation means that an enterprising 15-year-old working 50 hours a week cannot be counted as being either employed or unemployed—as the person is simply defined as not being in the labor force.

What Does It Take To Be Unemployed?

Well, we already know that a person does not have to do too much work to be considered as being *employed*—in fact all a person has to do is to be part of the civilian labor force and receive some pay for any part of the survey week that includes the 12th day of the month, or work for at least 15 hours in a family business for no pay during that period.

To be defined as *unemployed,* a person would have to be in the civilian labor force and jobless during the survey week. In addition, the person would have to be both available and looking for work. Specifically, the person would have to have made at least one specific effort to find a job during the month preceding the survey week.

How Do We Get the Unemployment Rate?

This is the easy part. After we determine the number of unemployed persons, we divide them by the size of the civilian labor force. The March 2009 numbers looked like this:

$$\text{Unemployment rate} = \frac{\text{number unemployed}}{\text{civilian labor force}} = \frac{13,161,000}{154,048,000} = 8.5\%$$

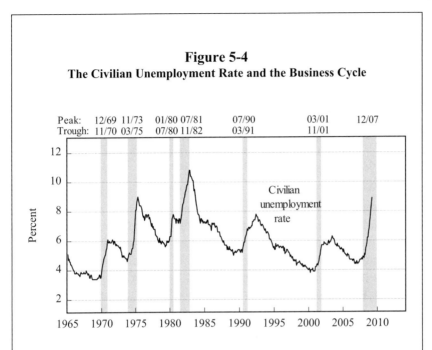

Figure 5-4
The Civilian Unemployment Rate and the Business Cycle

The unemployment rate acts like a leading indicator by turning up before a recession gets underway. Unfortunately, unemployment tends to increase fairly rapidly once a recession begins. After the recession is over, it usually takes several years for the rate to come back down to its former level.

Since the monthly survey data also identify the unemployed by sex, race, age, and marital status, we could also get the unemployment rate for adult men, adult women, teenagers, whites, blacks, and Hispanics. Unemployment rates for these groups are normally reported along with the overall civilian unemployment rate.

What About the Historical Record?

One of the more interesting things about the unemployment rate is that it tends to vary considerably with the state of the economy. For example, whenever the economy is in a period of expansion, and represented by the unshaded areas in Figure 5-4, the unemployment rate tends to fall—and somewhat slowly at that.

However, when the economy is about to enter a recession (represented by the shaded areas), the unemployment rate moves up rapidly. Indeed, one of the major concerns of economists is the speed at which the unemployment rate can climb. For example, if you look again at Figure 5-4 you can see that whenever the economy has entered a recession the unemployment rate has increased from a little more than 2 percent to as much as 5½ percent.

Are Unemployment Numbers Really All That Significant?

More than you might think! Even a relatively small change in the monthly unemployment rate involves a large number of people. For example, with a civilian labor force of 154,048,000, an increase in the unemployment rate of just one-tenth of 1 percent would mean that an additional 154,048 individuals would be out of work. This is more than the total number of people currently living in Bangor ME, Iowa City IA, Punta Gorda FL, Decatur AL, Madera CA, or Billings MT!

Incidentally, we might point out that the unemployment rate in the United States is measured differently than in many other nations. In the United States, we make an effort to look for the unemployed. In many other countries, people are not even counted as being unemployed until they actually show up to collect an unemployment check—which results in the unemployment rate being understated in those nations.

Have We Accounted for Everyone?

Not quite. Some individuals are marginally attached to the labor force. These are people who wanted to work, and were even available for work but had stopped looking for jobs sometime during the past 12 months. Others are *discouraged workers* who have stopped looking for jobs specifically because they believed no jobs were available for them.[5]

These two groups are neither employed nor unemployed—instead, they are simply not part of the labor. In reality, marginally attached and discouraged workers are fairly common, especially during periods of recession or in areas where homelessness is high.

---

[5] In March 2009, there were approximately 685,000 "discouraged workers."

The Unemployment Rate in Perspective

Aside from the pain, suffering, and sheer waste of resources implicit in the index, the unemployment rate has considerable value as an indicator of future economic activity. Although the warning period is relatively short, the series tends to be a reliable leading indicator of future economic downturns and a lagging indicator of impending recoveries.

Because it affects so many people, and because the unemployment rate is so difficult to bring down once it has risen sharply, it is also one of the most closely watched series in the economy.

Civilian Unemployment Rate	
Indicator status:	Leading for recessions; lagging for recoveries
Compiled by:	Bureau of Labor Statistics
Frequency:	Monthly
Release date:	Normally the first Friday of the following month
Revisions:	Monthly numbers not revised; annual revisions every January for the past 5 years to account for seasonal factors
Published data:	*Economic Indicators,* Council of Economic Advisors *The Employment Situation,* Bureau of Labor Statistics
Internet:	http://www.bls.gov http://www.EconSources.com

New Jobless Claims

The Employment and Training Administration (ETA) in the U.S. Department of Labor has a useful economic indicator called *initial unemployment insurance weekly claims*—although it is more commonly called "new jobless claims" or "initial unemployment claims." Basically the data cover new unemployment insurance claims that are generated at the state level and are then published as part of a combined federal/state program.

The data are published weekly by the ETA in both seasonally adjusted and unadjusted formats. Because the weekly numbers are subject to such wide variations, the data are smoothed with a 4-week moving average. The smoothed data series is shown in Figure 5-5.

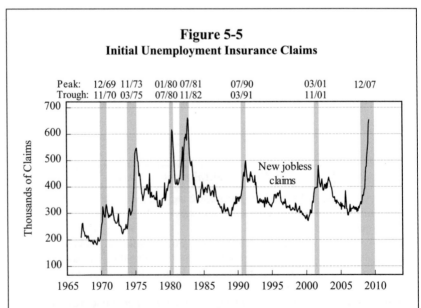

Figure 5-5
Initial Unemployment Insurance Claims

New unemployment insurance claims are released weekly by the Department of Labor. Because unemployment claims often vary dramatically from one week to the next, a 4-week moving average is employed to smooth the data.

Are New Jobless Claims an Economic Indicator?

Since labor is a variable cost, meaning that the number of workers employed varies with changes in the level of production, new claims for unemployment insurance are intuitively appealing as an economic indicator.

Indeed, Figure 5-5 shows that new claims tend to decline during expansionary periods and then rise sharply several months before the recession actually begins. This behavior makes the series a *leading* indicator when it comes to forecasting peaks in economic activity. The series also tends to decline when the recession ends, which makes it a *coincident* indicator when it comes to recoveries. Because of the relatively uniform lead times for the turning points, The Conference Board includes the series as one of the ten components for its *leading economic index (LEI)*.

We must remember, however, that the 4-week moving average is the important part of the statistic, not just the individual weekly numbers that are generally reported by the press. Because weekly data tend to vary so widely from one period to the next, we want to focus on the underlying trend if we want to get a better measure of labor market conditions.[6]

New Jobless Claims	
Indicator status:	Leading for recessions; coincident for recoveries
Compiled by:	Employment & Training Administration, Dept. of Labor
Frequency:	Weekly
Release date:	Advance figure, week after close of the last reporting week
Revisions:	Previous 2 weeks revised with each weekly release; annual revisions in January for several years back
Published data:	*Economic Indicators*, Council of Economic Advisors *Unemployment Insurance Weekly Claims Report*, Employment and Training Administration, U.S. Department of Labor
Internet:	http://www.dol.gov/opa/media/press/eta/ui/current.htm http://www.EconSources.com

---

[6] Some states tie people's jobless payments to earnings in a base period such as the previous quarter. This often causes people to delay unemployment filings until a more favorable base period can be reported.

Help-Wanted Advertising

Economic statistics, like the economy itself, are sometimes in transition. In fact, one of the more useful statistics designed to track job market conditions—the ***help-wanted advertising in newspapers*** series—is in a state of transition. The monthly newspaper index was compiled by The Conference Board and is available from 1951 to July 2008 with 1987 used as the base year. As can be seen in Figure 5-6 the series did a reasonably good job predicting recessions by turning down well in advance of the general economic downturn.

How Was the Newspaper Index Compiled?

To get the index, The Conference Board collected data on the number of help-wanted classified ads printed in 51 cities around the country. In each city, a count of all classified ads was taken from a single newspaper, and the total was adjusted for both seasonal patterns and the number of days in each calendar month.[7] The count for each city was then weighted according to the size of the labor market in the region and, after some other minor adjustments, compiled and released. The index was available both in a "national" format, shown in Figure 5-6, and for each of our nine census regions.

What About Its Value as an Indicator?

In general, the monthly help-wanted index tended to be a fairly reliable leading indicator when it comes to predicting the end of an expansion. The index tended to peak several months before the recession set in, and the amount of lead time was fairly consistent. It tended to fall throughout the recession and then bottom out just as, or shortly after, the recession ended. Finally, the data were normally not subject to revision, which means that we did not have to wait for additional data to see how a particular month fared.

---

[7] See *The Help-Wanted Index: Technical Description and Behavioral Trends*, Conference Board Report No. 716.

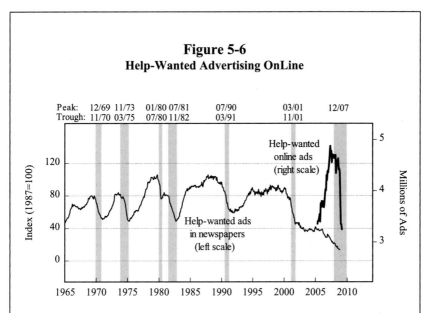

Figure 5-6
Help-Wanted Advertising OnLine

The Help-Wanted Advertising Index was based on the number of classified ads in 51 selected cities. Historically, the index has been a fairly reliable leading indicator of impending economic downturns.

The Help-Wanted OnLine Data Series

By the mid 1990s, as can be seen in Figure 5-6 something was happening to cause a significant change in the behavior of the index. The Internet, of course, along with changes in people's job search behavior, was thought to be the reason. After all, when someone wanted a job they could search a company's website, or they simply searched for a job on one of the many job search sites that were available on the web. Of course some people still consulted the local paper for employment opportunities, but in general the Internet was changing people's job search habits.

In response to this behavioral and structural change, The Conference Board decided to develop a similar series, only this time it would focus exclusively on help-wanted ads that appeared online rather than in newspapers. Thus the new series—***The Conference Board Help-Wanted Online Data Series (HWOL)***—was born. This new measure counts the number of new jobs and jobs reposted from the previous month that appear on more than 1,200 job sites.

Because the new HWOL series started in May 2005, the series has too short a history to fairly evaluate it as a reliable economic indicator. In addition, the data are collected by a private firm that uses proprietary data mining technologies; so details regarding the survey methodology and data aggregation are unknown.[8] Even so, the early results are promising.

For example, online help-wanted ads, or online job demand as it is also called, peaked at nearly 5 million in May 2007 and then dropped to slightly more than 3 million by March of 2009. Because the 2007 peak occurred approximately 18 months before the NBER's official December 2008 peak in overall economic activity, we can say that it has behaved as a leading economic indicator for the most recent recession. Whether it continues to predict recessions in the future, and how it performs with regard to economic recoveries, is yet to be known.

Help-Wanted OnLine Advertising	
Indicator status:	Leading indicator for the 2008-09 recession
Compiled by:	The Conference Board, 845 Third Avenue, New York, NY 10022
Frequency:	Monthly
Release date:	Normally the 1st Monday after the close of the reference month; occasionally *on* the last Monday during the reference month
Revisions:	Methodology not disclosed
Published data:	Monthly Conference Board press releases
Internet:	http://www.conference-board.org/ http://www.EconSources.com

---

[8] The company is WANTED Technologies Corporation, a leading supplier of real-time sales and business intelligence for the online media and recruitment industries.

Chapter 6

SPENDING, PROFITS, and EXPECTATIONS

Consumer Spending

Spending by consumers is often considered to be an important measure of the economy's health. Consumer spending is tracked by the U.S. Department of Commerce and is reported on a monthly basis in both current and constant (chained) dollars. As can be seen in Table 6-1, it is also the largest single component of GDP, accounting for more than two-thirds of all expenditures.

However, if you look in the Department of Commerce's index to current statistics, you won't find it listed under "consumer" or even "spending." Instead, it is called *personal consumption expenditures* and it is part of the national income and product accounts (NIPA).

How Does Consumer Spending Behave?

It turns out that the category of personal consumption expenditures is the most stable component of the economy.[1] Because of its stability and because the initial release from the Department of Commerce is in current dollars, the series generally tends to go up, regardless of whether the economy is expanding or not.

To illustrate, 531 months of current and real personal consumption expenditures are shown in Figure 6-1. During this period, the current dollar series turned down only 61 times—and only 21 of these monthly declines occurred during recessions!

---

[1] The reader may want to refer to Table 4-1 on page 61 to see how personal consumption expenditures vary with respect to other NIPA components.

We get a better view of spending when the series is adjusted for inflation by using constant dollars, but even then spending is relatively stable. The notable exception is the most recent recession which had 8 monthly declines during the first 16 months of the recession that began in December of 2007.

Of course the recession appeared to be at least half over when this book went to press in May 2009, so the series will probably go down even more before the recovery begins. The point, however, is that personal consumption expenditures have been historically resilient regardless of the state of the economy.

Table 6-1
Personal Consumption Expenditures, Billions of Dollars

	Current	Constant (2000$)	% GDP
Gross domestic product	*$14,075*	*$11,340.9*	*100.0*
Personal consumption expenditures	*9,955.7*	*8,214.2*	*70.7*
Durable goods	963.8	1,133.9	6.8
Motor vehicles and parts	338.6	350.6	2.4
Furniture and household equipment	398.0	608.5	2.8
Other	227.2	219.6	1.6
Nondurable goods	2,810.8	2,326.2	20.0
Food	1,382.1	1,066.9	9.8
Clothing and shoes	368.7	406.1	2.6
Gasoline and oil	243.9	178.4	1.7
Fuel oil and coal	24.3	12.4	0.2
Other	791.8	685.1	5.6
Services	6,181.1	4,746.5	43.9
Housing	1,535.5	1,185.2	10.9
Household operation	568.2	429.1	4.0
Electricity and gas	239.8	154.5	1.7
Other household operations	328.4	275.6	2.3
Transportation	371.5	288.4	2.6
Medical care	1,835.0	1,396.0	13.0
Recreation	417.9	333.2	3.0
Other	1,453.1	1,112.1	10.3
Gross private domestic investment	*1,579.8*	*1,329.8*	*11.2*
Net exports of goods and services	*-337.7*	*-308.4*	*-2.4*
Government consumption & gross investment	*2,877.7*	*2,073.8*	*20.4*

Source: BEA, first quarter advance 2009 estimates

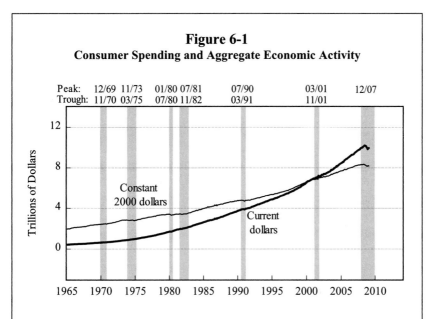

Figure 6-1
Consumer Spending and Aggregate Economic Activity

Personal consumption expenditures are among the most predictable of all economic statistics, especially when measured in current dollars. A constant dollar measure gives a better picture of spending, but it too reflects the remarkable stability of consumer spending.

So, if personal consumption expenditures are so stable, and therefore predictable, why do we hear so much about it? Perhaps the reason is simply that the series is available, or perhaps it is because the series is too large to ignore. The series does give us an idea of what is happening in the consumer sector, but it does not exhibit the type of behavior that helps us predict changes in future economic activity.

Personal Consumption Expenditures

Indicator status:	None
Compiled by:	Bureau of Economic Analysis
Frequency:	Monthly
Release date:	End of month on the day following release of GDP
Revisions:	Revisions of estimates to beginning of previous quarter
Published data:	*Survey of Current Business*, U.S. Department of Commerce
Internet:	http://www.bea.gov
	http://www.EconSources.com

Retail Sales

In order to collect data on retail sales, the Census Bureau conducts a monthly retail trade survey that covers approximately 5,000 retail and food service firms. The first estimate of retail sales is published in a series called *advance monthly sales for retail trade and food services* and appears about two weeks after the close of the reference month. The series is revised two more times before the numbers become final, but the advance sales get the attention because they come out first. Breakdowns are available for a variety of industries, including building materials, automotive dealers, grocery stores, eating and drinking establishments, and many others.[2]

The Historical Record

This series is important because it covers about 65 percent of total national sales. The advance release of monthly retail sales data is not adjusted for inflation, although constant dollar data are available shortly thereafter. The U.S. Census Bureau has also been reporting on retail E-commerce sales since 2000, although the data are not shown in Figure 6-2.

For the most part, the data reflect discretionary expenditures of the consumer sector, as well as some spending at retail establishments by governmental and business units. Consumers are often reluctant to reduce spending until they are forced to, which typically happens right after a recession begins. Normally this reluctance to spend does not seem to last long, although the most recent recession that began in December of 2007 is an obvious, if not remarkable, exception.

The good news is that consumer spending normally starts to pick up before the economy recovers, making the series a leading indicator for recoveries. This feature is more clearly evident when the

---

[2] The retail sales series is different from most NIPA data in that the monthly sales figures are not annualized. Instead, the monthly numbers report on sales for the period and annual sales are determined by adding up the sales for each of the individual months. The series is, however, adjusted for seasonal, holiday, and trading day differences.

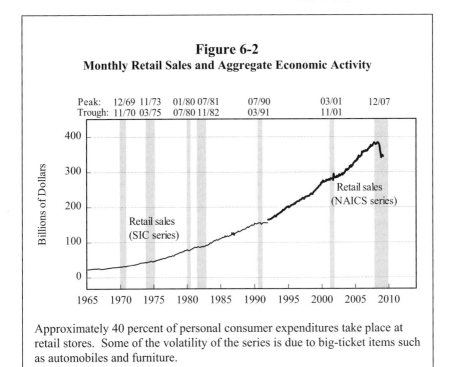

Figure 6-2
Monthly Retail Sales and Aggregate Economic Activity

Peak: 12/69 11/73   01/80 07/81   07/90   03/01   12/07
Trough: 11/70 03/75   07/80 11/82   03/91   11/01

Approximately 40 percent of personal consumer expenditures take place at retail stores. Some of the volatility of the series is due to big-ticket items such as automobiles and furniture.

current dollar sales are converted to constant dollars, but current figures are shown because they appear first and therefore get most of the attention.[3]

Monthly Retail Sales	
Indicator status:	Leading for recoveries
Compiled by:	Census Bureau
Frequency:	Monthly
Release date:	Approximately two weeks after the close of the month
Revisions:	Advance, preliminary, final estimates released monthly
Published data:	*Economic Indicators*, Council of Economic Advisors
	Advance Monthly Retail Sales, U.S. Dept of Commerce
Internet:	http://www.census.gov/econ/www/retmenu.html
	http://www.EconSources.com

---

[3] The two series shown in Figure 6-2 are the result of the Commerce Department's switch from the older Standard Industrial Classification (SIC) to the newer North American Industrial Classification System (NAICS). The switch affected the number of firms in the survey, and hence the volume of sales covered. This conversion to NAICS will eventually affect most industry-based statistics.

Wholesale Sales

The monthly sales of merchant wholesalers, more commonly known as *monthly wholesale sales*, provide yet another view of aggregate economic activity. Unfortunately, the story they tell is not always clear because the numbers tend to fluctuate considerably.

Constructing the Survey

Monthly wholesale sales are derived from the monthly Wholesale Trade Survey conducted by the U.S. Census Bureau. The mail-out/mail-back survey covers approximately 4,000 wholesale firms that are primarily engaged in wholesale trade (jobbers, industrial distributors, exporters, importers, and others who take title to the goods they sell). Manufacturing firms that sell directly to the retailer, merchandise or commodity brokers, and merchants that work on commission are excluded.

The most recent figures are "preliminary" and are released 6 weeks after the close of the reference month. "Final" figures are released at the same time for the month preceding the reference month. Finally, all of the series are revised annually.

Why the Interest in Wholesale Sales?

We're not entirely sure, except for the fact that the series does report on an important segment of the economy—essentially the segment covered by the survey. It may also be due to the assumption that whatever happens to retailers will also happen to wholesalers, but the pattern is less clear given the fact that downturns in the wholesale sales series sometimes leads, sometimes lags, and at other times is coincident with the beginning of a recession. When it comes to the ensuing recovery, the wholesale series is sometimes coincident with, and at other times lags, the economic expansion.

Despite the inability to forecast the turning points, we should note that it does perform fairly well as a coincident indicator, and

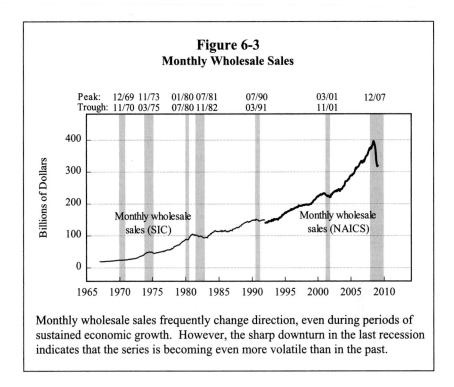

Figure 6-3
Monthly Wholesale Sales

Monthly wholesale sales frequently change direction, even during periods of sustained economic growth. However, the sharp downturn in the last recession indicates that the series is becoming even more volatile than in the past.

certainly the remarkable collapse in 2008-09 closely mirrors the decline in retail sales. The series may well have other uses, but none as an indicator of future business cycle turning points.

Monthly Wholesale Sales	
Indicator status:	No status with regard to future economic activity
Compiled by:	Census Bureau
Frequency:	Monthly
Release date:	Six weeks after the close of the reference month
Revisions:	Preliminary estimates are converted to final estimates after one month; annual revisions; benchmark revisions every few years.
Published data:	*Monthly Wholesale Trade*, Census Bureau
	Economic Indicators, Council of Economic Advisors
Internet:	http://www.census.gov/wholesale/index.html
	http://www.EconSources.com

Employment Cost Index

The quarterly *employment cost index* (ECI) is a newer series designed to measure the change in the cost of labor over time. The series includes wages, salaries, and the employer's cost of employee benefits at approximately 13,400 private business and 1,900 government establishments. The measure dates from 1982, and it has a wide following because it provides a measure of the change in the cost of labor that is free from the influence of employment shifts that takes place among occupations and industries.[4]

Like most other series, we can focus on the level of the index, or changes in the level. A popular version, shown in Figure 6-4, is in terms of percentage changes of quarterly data, although percentage changes over 12-month periods are also available.

Uses and Users of the ECI

Because the ECI reflects employment cost trends, and because the cost of labor is such a large component of production, it is often used in escalator clauses. The federal government uses the series to adjust defense contracts, and it is even used to determine allowable increases in Medicare hospital charges.

The series has been used in numerous private and public sector collective bargaining agreements—including the District of Columbia, Baltimore, and Los Angeles. Federal pay adjustments for the U.S. Congress, federal judges, and senior government officials are also tied to the ECI, as are the salaries of many state officials.

Finally, the Federal Reserve System uses the ECI as an indicator of future inflation—as a tool to help predict where we are headed, rather than to tell us where we have been. In fact, the Fed seldom raises the discount rate without voicing some concern over increases in current or expected future labor costs.

---

[4] Technical Note, "Employment Cost Index—March 2009," Bureau of Labor Statistics News, U.S. Department of Labor.

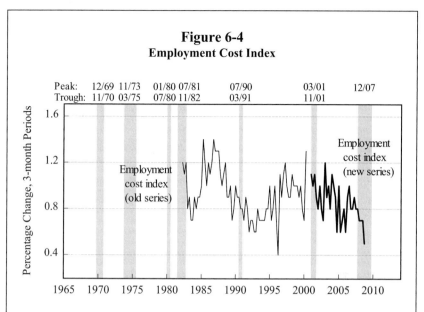

Figure 6-4
Employment Cost Index

The employment cost index, available only since 1982, is used as an escalator to adjust national defense contracts and federal pay scales. It is thought to be an indicator of future inflation and is closely watched by the Fed. It has no properties as an indicator of future changes in aggregate economic activity.

The National Compensation Survey (NCS)

The quarterly ECI is part of the NCS that provides data on employment costs, occupational compensation and employee benefits. While the ECI has no value as an indicator of future changes in GDP, it is our best overall indicator of the cost of labor and possibly future inflationary pressures.

Employment Cost Index	
Indicator status:	No status with regard to future economic activity
Compiled by:	Bureau of Labor Statistics
Frequency:	Quarterly
Release date:	End of the month following the reference quarter
Revisions:	To be revised as part of the National Compensation Survey
Published data:	*Employment Cost Index,* Department of Labor
	Economic Indicators, Council of Economic Advisors
Internet:	http://www.bls.gov/news.release/pdf/eci.pdf
	http://www.EconSources.com

Corporate Profits

The Bureau of Economic Analysis in the Department of Commerce compiles several series on corporate profits. Total profits are reported for domestic financial and nonfinancial firms, with the latter including estimates for manufacturing, trade, transportation and public utilities. The most important is *corporate profits after tax*.[5]

The Historical Record

We think of the net corporate profits series as being an indicator of the general financial health of the corporate sector. Indeed, this is exactly what the series is intended to measure, even if it does not receive the same lavish attention the press gives to the most recent IBM, General Motors, or Microsoft earnings reports. The quarterly series is part of the GDP accounts and is released seven times a year, with the first release occurring approximately 45 days after the close of the quarter. The second is a final estimate that is based on more complete data and is released approximately 90 days after the close of the quarter.[6]

Good, But Hard to Find

The leading indicator properties of corporate profits after tax are shown in Figure 6-5. In fact, with the exception of the 1973-74 recession, corporate profits have stalled or turned down well in advance of the general decline in economic activity.

When we hear about "corporate profits" in the news, the reference frequently is to the quarterly earnings report of one or more

---

[5] For a comprehensive discussion of the difference between NIPA and regular business profits, see Kenneth Petrick's "Comparing NIPA Profits with S&P 500 Profits," *Survey of Current Business*, April 2001. The differences are too numerous to elaborate here.

[6] With the exception of the fourth quarter preliminary estimate, corporate profits are released along with the preliminary and final—but not the advance—GDP estimates. This means that the series is released seven times a year; three times with the preliminary GDP estimates, and four times with the final GDP estimates.

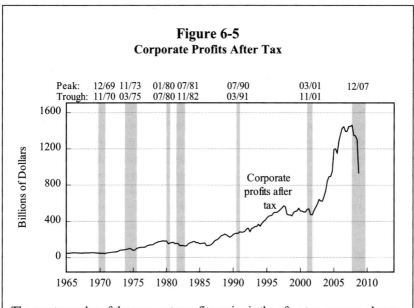

Figure 6-5
Corporate Profits After Tax

Peak:	12/69	11/73	01/80 07/81	07/90		03/01	12/07
Trough:	11/70	03/75	07/80 11/82	03/91		11/01	

The most popular of the corporate profits series is the after-tax measure shown above. Because data are collected from quarterly corporate reports, the series is only available quarterly, and then after a considerable delay.

individual companies—not the comprehensive series in Figure 6-5. As for its value to the casual observer, the main limitation is that it is buried in the GDP accounts, and it is reported on a delayed and somewhat irregular basis.

Corporate Profits

Indicator status:	Leading indicator for recessions; coincident for recoveries
Compiled by:	Bureau of Economic Analysis
Frequency:	Seven times a year
Release date:	Approximately 45 days following the close of the quarter
Revisions:	A second, final, revision appears 45 days after the first, or 90 days after the end of the quarter
Published data:	*Economic Indicators,* Council of Economic Advisors
	Survey of Current Business, U.S. Department of Commerce
Internet:	http://www.bea.gov
	http://www.EconSources.com

Consumer Expectations and Confidence

Because the consumer sector makes up such a large portion of the overall economy, it is reasonable to assume that people's decisions to save or spend can be affected by the expectations and confidence they have in the economy or in their own financial situation. These considerations are important, and two highly regarded series are designed to track these factors.

Consumer Expectations

The first of the two series is derived from a "consumer sentiment" survey compiled by the Institute for Social Research (ISR) at the University of Michigan. The survey is based on a random monthly sample of 500 people selected from all states except Alaska and Hawaii. The sample is closed, which means that only the individuals initially selected for the sample are contacted for the survey. Because of the design, a new group of consumers appears in the sample every month.[7]

The survey covers five major categories reported as separate indices: personal finance, current and expected; business conditions, current and expected; and buying conditions. The results of the survey are compiled and made available for release no later than the first week of the following month.[8]

One of the subcomponents of the survey is the ***index of consumer expectations*** shown in Figure 6-6. Historically the index

---

[7] According to Richard T. Curtin at the Survey Research Center, "The sample is designed to maximize the study of change by incorporating a rotating panel sample design in an ongoing monthly survey program. For each monthly sample, an independent cross-section sample of households is drawn. The respondents chosen in this drawing are then reinterviewed six months later. A rotating panel design results in the total sample for any one survey is normally made up of 55% new respondents, and 45% being reviewed for the second time." *Surveys of Consumers*, Survey Research Center.

[8] The monthly reports are available on a subscription basis. For further information contact Surveys of Consumers, Survey Research Center, University of Michigan, 426 Thompson Street, Ann Arbor, MI, 48104-2321.

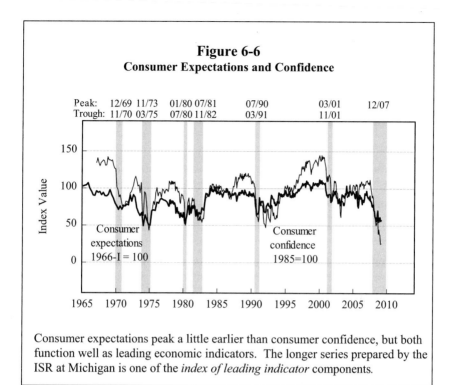

Figure 6-6
Consumer Expectations and Confidence

Consumer expectations peak a little earlier than consumer confidence, but both function well as leading economic indicators. The longer series prepared by the ISR at Michigan is one of the *index of leading indicator* components.

performed so well as a leading indicator of future economic activity that it was included as one of the individual components in The Conference Board's composite *leading economic index*.

Consumer Confidence

In 1967, The Conference Board introduced its own ***consumer confidence survey***.[9] This survey takes place during the first 2 weeks of every month and covers 5,000 households. Data are then compiled and released during the third week of the same month.

Consumer confidence is expressed as an index with a base of 1985=100, and it covers a number of categories, including appraisals of the current business situation; expectations of business conditions, employment, and income for the next six months; plans to buy

---

[9] See the *Consumer Confidence Survey*, a monthly report from the Consumer Research Center at The Conference Board, 845 Third Ave, New York, NY 10022. The Conference Board also compiles the *index of leading indicators*.

automobiles, homes, and major appliances in the next six months; and questions on vacation plans. The index is available on a regional basis and is also broken down by age of household head and by household income.

Looking Ahead

Both series are important leading indicators, turning down before the economy peaks, and turning up before the economy recovers. If anything, the index of consumer expectations tends to peak somewhat earlier than the confidence measure, and it tends to recover somewhat earlier as well. Both series are widely followed, and both are used to forecast impending economic developments.

Perhaps the most important difference between the two series is accessibility. Both series are available on a subscription basis to users, but only The Conference Board issues monthly press releases with the latest numbers.[10] As a result, the monthly numbers we hear about in the press are usually The Conference Board's consumer confidence series.

Consumer Expectations and Confidence	
Indicator status:	Both series are leading for recessions and recoveries
Compiled by:	*Consumer Confidence,* The Conference Board
	Consumer Expectations, Institute for Social Research, University of Michigan
Frequency:	Monthly (both)
Release date:	Latter part of reference month (both)
Published data:	*Consumer Confidence Survey,* subscription from The Conference Board
	Consumer Expectations, subscription basis from ISR
Internet:	http://www.conference-board.org/economics/indicators.cfm
	http://www.src.isr.umich.edu/
	http://www.EconSources.com

---

[10] The monthly number for consumer expectations is normally available from The Conference Board on its website. Otherwise, the data on the ISR website are several months old.

Beige Book

There are any number of economic statistics that affect our daily lives. Most, like GDP, industrial production, and the unemployment rate, are statistics in the true sense of the word. Others, like "new jobs created," are more like numbers than statistical series, although they are often reported as if they really were.

The Beige Book, the summary of economic conditions and collection of anecdotal information that is prepared by the Fed, fits into this category. The report is released eight times a year, and—because it appears two weeks prior to the Fed's monetary policy meetings—it is often treated as if it were a guide to what the Fed intends to do. The reality is much different.

The Demise of Discretionary Fiscal Policy

Discretionary fiscal policy, our federal government's taxing and spending behavior, has become so politically driven and so cumbersome in its application that it cannot respond very effectively to rapid changes in economic conditions. As a result, we rely more on programs that are more or less fixed, such as progressive income tax rates, unemployment insurance compensation, welfare subsidies, and other such programs that economists call automatic stabilizers.

Of course, in times of serious economic crises, such as in the 2008-09 recession, government fiscal policies become more attractive despite their cumbersome and politically complex nature. However, it remains to be seen if they are effective and efficient.

The Fed and Monetary Policy

Trying to get a handle on what is going to happen in the American economy today is often considered largely synonymous with trying to figure out what the Federal Reserve System is going to do. However, the execution of monetary policy is the easy part because the Fed only has to increase or decrease the size of the money supply in order to affect the availability and cost of credit. The laws of supply and demand reign supreme here: increase the money supply, and interest rates go down; reduce or tighten the money supply, and rates go up.[11]

Monetary Policy Decision Variables

The hard part of monetary policy is usually to decide which way to go. For example, when the economy was mired in recession in 2009, the Fed was confronted with the choice between continued monetary expansion to maintain lower interest rates, or to rein in the money supply in hopes of preventing inflation later on.

The policy makers at the Fed certainly watch all of the statistics explored in this book, but they also want to know as much as possible about other economic conditions that are more difficult to quantify. Besides, the Fed has a long tradition of considering the regional viewpoints of its twelve district banks before it makes its monetary policy decisions. As a result, by 1970 these regional summaries were formalized in a confidential—for policymakers only—report called *The Red Book*.[12]

By the early 1980s, however, Congress was pressing the Fed to be more open with respect to its monetary policy making. The result was the release of *The Red Book* to the public in 1983. To mark this change, the cover of the report was changed to beige, hence what is known today as *The Beige Book*.

The modern report is approximately 30-40 pages long and draws on a variety of information from the board of directors at the Fed's twelve district banks, branch bank directors, contacts in the business community, and so on. A summary of national economic conditions, shown in Figure 6-7, makes up the first part of *The Beige Book*. Summaries of economic conditions in each of the twelve districts make up the remainder. There are no statistical tables in the report.

---

[11] Assuming *ceteris paribus* of course, the assumption that all other things remain constant while the money supply changes.

[12] See David Fettig, Arthur J. Rolnick, and David E. Runkle, "The Federal Reserve's Beige Book, A Better Mirror than Crystal Ball," *The Region*, Federal Reserve Bank of Minneapolis, March 1999, for an excellent history and summary (the article can be retrieved from either of the two websites listed at the end of this section).

Figure 6-7
The Beige Book – Summary of Commentary of
Current Economic Conditions by Federal Reserve District

Reports from the Federal Reserve Banks indicate that overall economic activity contracted further or remained weak. However, five of the twelve Districts noted a moderation in the pace of decline, and several saw signs that activity in some sectors was stabilizing at a low level.

Manufacturing activity weakened across a broad range of industries in most Districts, with only a few exceptions. Nonfinancial service activity continued to contract across Districts. Retail spending remained sluggish, although some Districts noted a slight improvement in sales compared with the previous reporting period. Residential real estate markets continued to be weak. Home prices and construction were still falling in most areas, but better-than-expected buyer traffic led to a scattered pickup in sales in a number of Districts. Nonresidential real estate conditions continued to deteriorate. Difficulty obtaining commercial real estate financing was constraining construction and investment activity. Spending on business travel declined as corporations cut back. Reports on tourism were mixed. Bankers reported tight credit conditions, rising delinquencies, and some deterioration of loan quality.

Agricultural conditions were generally favorable across Districts, although drought conditions persisted in the Dallas and San Francisco Districts. The Districts reporting on energy said reduced demand, high inventories, and lower prices led to steep cutbacks in oil and natural gas drilling and production activity. The Minneapolis, Kansas City, and Dallas Districts noted declines in employment in the oil and gas extraction industry.

The above *Beige Book* summary was prepared by the Federal Reserve Bank of Dallas and was made public two weeks prior to the April 28-29 monetary policy meeting in 2009. The Fed cautions that the Beige Book comments are commentaries only, and not the official views of the Fed.

Source: *Beige Book*, April 15, 2009

The summary in Figure 6-7 goes on to describe conditions in the areas of consumer spending, real estate and construction, manufacturing, banking and finance, insurance, labor markets, and agriculture and natural resources. If that doesn't leave you bleary-eyed, you can pursue the full 36 pages of similar commentary at the regional level.[13]

---

[13] We have never, in fact, met a single living economist outside the Fed who has read any of the *Beige Books* from beginning to end.

Mirror or Crystal Ball?

The question facing Fed watchers is the extent to which the Beige Book provides us with an insight into the Fed's likely intentions. Do statements such as "Most Districts continued to report weakness in labor markets and some downward pressure on wages, although benefit costs continued to increase" mean that the Fed will change interest rates?

Fed economists have tried to answer this question by assigning numerical scores to various aspects of more than 300 *Beige Books* published since 1970. The scores were then analyzed to see if they could improve on the estimates given by the computerized forecasting models already used by the Fed. One study found that *The Beige Book* was of some help. Another, and more complete, study found that a close examination of *The Beige Book* could not improve on the quality of output already provided by private sector forecasts. According to the latter, "the media and Fed watchers would do well to put aside *The Beige Book* and focus on private sector forecasts in their attempts to predict monetary policy."[14]

So, why bother with *The Beige Book*? For one, any given report is quite detailed and generally covers important regional developments in labor markets, agricultural outlook, industrial production, the retail trades, and so on: just the kinds of things that are not always well revealed by statistics. For another, we hear about it in the press often enough to realize that we should know more about it. Finally, it is nice to know some of what the Fed knows—even if the product is more of a mirror than a crystal ball.

The Beige Book

Indicator status:	None
Compiled by:	The Federal Reserve District Banks
Frequency:	Eight times per year
Release date:	Two weeks preceding the Fed's FOMC meeting
Published data:	*The Beige Book*, The Federal Reserve Board of Governors
Internet:	http://www.federalreserve.gov/
	http://www.EconSources.com

---

[14] Fettig, et al. "The Federal Reserve's Beige Book," *The Region*, 1999. This article describes both studies in more detail.

Chapter 7

PRICES, MONEY, and INTEREST RATES

Consumer Price Index

The consumer price index, or CPI, is one of the most comprehensive statistical measures compiled by the Bureau of Labor Statistics. In fact, the BLS actually computes two measures. The first, and most important, is the *CPI for all urban consumers (CPI-U)*, which covers about 87 percent of the total population. The second, which overlaps the first, is the *CPI for urban wage earners and clerical workers (CPI-W)* and covers about 32 percent of the population. CPI data are released about two weeks after the close of the reference month.

Each index is a measure of the average change in prices for a fixed "market basket" of goods and services used by consumers. It is not, however, the same as a cost-of-living index because it does not take into account all of the factors that would allow one to maintain the same standard of living with a given level of expenditures.[1]

Constructing the Sample

The CPI uses a market basket of goods and services that consumers typically bought during a 2005-06 base period. From this,

---

[1] Missing from the analysis are such things as the impact of government regulations on our lives, environmental factors, even things like crime, health, and water quality. When asked by a Congressional advisory committee to establish a cost-of-living index as the primary objective of the CPI, the BLS response was that "if the BLS staff or other technical experts knew how to produce a true cost-or-living index on a monthly production schedule, that would be what we would produce." See "Consumer Price Indexes: Short Term Recommendations," on the 1998 CPI Revisions BLS website.

the BLS constructed a list of eight major product groups (PGs) which were broken down into approximately 70 expenditure classes (ECs), nearly 200 strata, and approximately 400 entry level items (ELIs) in the manner illustrated in Figure 7-1. Approximately 80,000 individual products were then selected as being representative ELI category items.

Table 7-1
Major Product Groups and Entry Level Sampling Items in the CPI

PG#1. Food and Beverages
      EC#1: Cereals and Bakery Products
          Strata #1: Cereals and cereal products
              ELI#1: *Flour and prepared flour mixes*
              ELI#2: *Breakfast cereal*
              ELI#3: *Rice, pasta, and corn meal*
          Strata #2: Bakery products
              ELI#1: *White bread*
              ELI#2: *Other bread*
          Strata #3: Fresh biscuits, rolls, muffins
PG#2. Housing
PG#3. Apparel
PG#4. Transportation
PG#5. Medical Care
PG#6. Recreation
PG#7. Education and Communication
PG#8. Other Goods and Services

Each of these 80,000 items is then priced and repriced all over again at regular monthly intervals. Because the final dollar value of an 80,000 item market basket would be so large, however, the new market basket prices are expressed as a percent of the base period prices.

To illustrate, when the CPI reached 212.7 in March 2009, it meant that the total market basket amounted to 212.7 percent of its base period cost, or that a typical item costing $1 in the 1982-84 base period cost $2.13 in March 2009. Market baskets are typically revised every 10 years or so, and the base year index is usually updated whenever the market basket is updated. However, the CPI is one of the few exceptions to this rule largely because so many CPI users were so familiar with, and had extensive records of, prices with the

1982-84 base period. As a result, new prices are reported as a percent of their 1982-84 base, while the market basket items making up the sample are based on 2005-06 consumer expenditure patterns.[2]

Estimating Inflation from the CPI

Because the CPI measures the level of prices, it does not directly measure inflation. However, inflation estimates can be derived by computing the change in the level of the CPI from one period to another. The one we often hear about is based on 1-month percentage changes in the CPI-U that are adjusted for seasonal variations and then annualized. Consumer prices are also reported for various other categories such as food and energy.

However, annualized estimates based on 1-month changes often result in relatively wide swings in the inflation rate, so it is generally preferable to compute the change over longer periods such as the 12-month spans shown in Figure 7-2. Another measure is the so-called "core" rate of inflation that does not include the more volatile food and energy price categories. The historical record shows that inflation tends to get worse in the latter stages of an expansion, but other than that, inflation has no value as an indicator of future economic activity.

Other Uses for the CPI

Even though the CPI is not a cost-of-living measure, it is often used as a surrogate. According to the BLS, the CPI affects the income of almost 80 million persons, including 48.4 million Social Security beneficiaries, about 19.8 million food stamp recipients, and 4.2 million military and federal Civil Service retirees and survivors. It is also used in escalator clauses for about 2 million workers covered by collective bargaining agreements. Changes in the CPI also affect more than 26.5 million children who eat school lunches, as well as the annual Federal income tax bracket adjustments.

---

[2] The choice of a base year is not that important because comparisons between any two years can be found by simply dividing two values of the CPI. If the CPI in April 2003 was 183.8, and if the CPI in March 1999 was 165.1, then April 2003 prices were 183.8/165.1 = 1.113, or 1.113 times higher than they were a year earlier. Alternatively, we could say that prices increased by 11.3 percent during the 12-month period. You can do the same for any other years. If the CPI in January 1997 was 159.4, and if it were 162.8 in May 1998, then prices increased 162.8/159.4 = 1.021 times over the 15-month period.

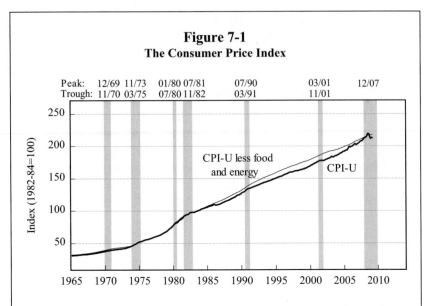

Figure 7-1
The Consumer Price Index

The consumer price index tells us little other than how the level of prices in one period compares to another. To find the rate of inflation, we have to compute, and then annualize, monthly or quarterly changes in the CPI.

The Politics of the CPI

Because of the enormous impact of the CPI, it is constantly under scrutiny. One was in 1996 when a special Congressional commission reported that the measure overestimated the annual cost of living by nearly 1.1 percent. At the time, the main culprit was the fixed market basket which had not been updated since 1982-1984. The problem, now fixed, was that the market basket did not account for the substitution effects that occur when consumers use one product rather than another, nor did it take into account changes in shopping patterns that occur when consumers shop at discount outlets. Finally, quality improvements to existing products such as VCRs and computers tended to get overlooked.

The commission also reported that a 1-percentage point annual reduction in the CPI would reduce the federal deficit by about $1 trillion over 12 years—savings due to lower cost-of-living payments to social security recipients, higher receipts from taxpayers as tax bracket adjustments become smaller, and lower costs of other federal

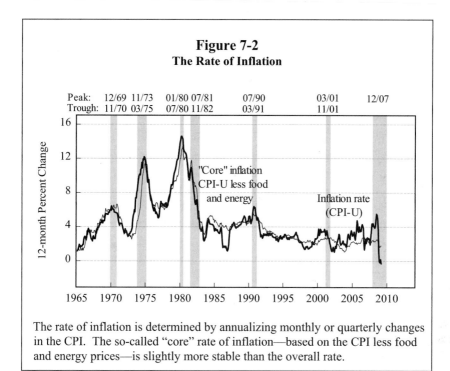

Figure 7-2
The Rate of Inflation

The rate of inflation is determined by annualizing monthly or quarterly changes in the CPI. The so-called "core" rate of inflation—based on the CPI less food and energy prices—is slightly more stable than the overall rate.

programs that are indexed by the CPI. This, of course, added a political element to the revision as the Federal government was struggling to balance its budget at the time.

The BLS did address some methodological issues, and the CPI is better for it. Even so, the CPI today is neither more nor less than it ever was: a measure of the average change over time in the prices paid by urban consumers for a market basket of consumer goods and services.

Consumer Price Index

Indicator status:	None
Compiled by:	Bureau of Labor Statistics
Frequency:	Monthly
Release date:	8th through 19th of the following month
Revisions:	Seasonal revisions in January for up to 5 years
Published data:	*Economic Indicators*, Council of Economic Advisors
	CPI Summary News Release, Bureau of Labor Statistics
Internet:	http://www.bls.gov/cpi
	http://www.EconSources.com

Producer Price Index

Another important price series is the ***producer price index (PPI)***, which measures average changes in selling prices received by domestic producers for their output. Until 1978 the series was known as the *wholesale price index*, but the title was changed to emphasize that the series measures only price changes between the producer and the *first* purchaser of the product. It does not measure price changes that occur between other intermediaries such as the final wholesaler and the retailer who buys the product for resale to the public.

Coverage and Reporting

Every month, over 100,000 price quotations are obtained from virtually every sector of the U.S. economy, including both goods and service industries. Price indices are then prepared for three major groups—finished goods, intermediate goods, and crude goods—with final reports made available for more than 10,000 individual products and product groups. The index series in the PPI are reported with 1982 = 100 as the base year.

The Historical Record

Figure 7-3 shows the level of the PPI for finished goods in comparison to the CPI (or CPI-U to be exact). The figure shows that there is a fairly close relationship between the two measures, although for several reasons the PPI has fallen behind in recent years. For one thing, the PPI measures price changes only when the original producer sells the product. If several intermediaries are involved after this sale takes place, the profit margins taken by each will drive up the final retail price. For another, the PPI does not cover imported items, as does the CPI.

Historically, most of the interest in producer prices has focused on their eventual impact on consumer prices. If prices go up at the factory, the reasoning goes, consumers will pay more later on.

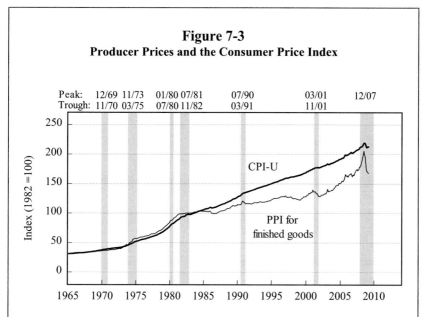

Figure 7-3
Producer Prices and the Consumer Price Index

Peak: 12/69 11/73   01/80 07/81   07/90   03/01   12/07
Trough: 11/70 03/75   07/80 11/82   03/91   11/01

The PPI has not kept pace with the CPI in recent years, in part because of differences in coverage between the two series. When changes in the PPI are plotted over 3- or 6-month spans, the series appears much like Figure 7-2, with prices rising late in the expansion and then slowing or declining shortly thereafter.

Increases in the PPI can lead to increases in the CPI, but for the reasons given above, the linkage is not as close as it once was. Percentage changes in the PPI for 1-month and 3-month spans can also be computed, but like the CPI, producer prices have no leading, lagging, or coincident indicator status.

Producer Price Index	
Indicator status:	None
Compiled by:	Bureau of Labor Statistics
Frequency:	Monthly
Release date:	Second week of the following month
Revisions:	Up to 4 months after the initial monthly release
Published data:	*PPI News Release*, Bureau of Labor Statistics
	Economic Indicators, Council of Economic Advisors
Internet:	http://www.bls.gov/ppi
	http://www.EconSources.com

Money Supply

Economists think of money as anything that serves as a unit of account, a medium of exchange, and a store of value. However, the exact definition of money is complicated by the fact that it takes so many different forms, ranging from coins to savings accounts to Eurodollar deposits.[3]

Definitions of Money

The Fed employs several definitions of money, two of which correspond to the functions of money described above.[4] One is called **M1** and is the transactional component of the money supply, or the part most closely identified with money's role as a medium of exchange. As can be seen in Table 7-2, this definition of the money supply includes coins, paper currency, traveler's checks, demand deposits, NOW accounts, credit union share drafts, and other checkable deposits.

If we want to consider money's role as a store of value as well as a medium of exchange, the definition is expanded to include other, and sometimes lesser known, forms of holding money. This broader-based definition of money is known as **M2**, and we get it by adding savings deposits (including money market deposit accounts), small-denomination time deposits, and retail money market funds to M1. These seven different components of M1 and M2 are shown in Table 7-2.

The Historical Record

Since the money supply is managed by the Federal Reserve System, we would expect that some variations in the money stock are possible over time. Figure 7-4 shows the levels of M1 and M2

---

[3] Dollar-denominated bank deposits in foreign countries, not necessarily in Europe.

[4] A total of four definitions—M1, M2, M3, and DEBT—are used by the Fed. See the *Federal Reserve Bulletin* for more on measures of M3 and DEBT.

Table 7-2
Components of the Money Supply, Billions of Current Dollars

1. Coins and paper currency	$844.9
2. Traveler's checks	5.4
3. Demand deposits	389.5
4. Other checkable deposits (NOW accounts, share drafts)	322.4
M1	**$1,562.2**
5. Savings deposits	
(includes money market deposit accounts)	4,375.7
6. Small denomination time deposits	
(includes retail repurchase agreements)	1,346.8
7. Retail money market funds	1,031.9
M2 = (M1 plus lines 5-7)	**$8,316.7**

Source: *Statistical Release H.6*, May 7, 2009, Federal Reserve Board of Governors

from 1965 to the present. According to the figure, both definitions of money tend to rise steadily over time, but without regard to changes in economic activity.

Is Money a Leading Economic Indicator?

It turns out that money, like any other commodity, can also be measured in terms of current or constant dollar amounts, the latter being preferable if we want to compensate for the distortions of inflation. If the two series shown in Figure 7-4 were converted to constant dollar amounts, they would both exhibit some leading indicator characteristics. In fact, M2 in constant dollars has historically been included in the *leading economic index (LEI)* that is now compiled by The Conference Board.[5]

The process of converting M1 or M2 to constant dollar measures is not difficult, but it is not done by the Fed—which is the reason that only current dollar amounts are shown here. Instead, the Fed only reports its money statistics in current terms, leaving the conversion to The Conference Board for its leading economic index.[6]

---

[5] The list of component series that make up the *LEI* is on page 54.

[6] One way to make the conversion is to divide M1 and M2 by the implicit price deflator for personal consumption expenditures, and then multiplied by 100. This is a legitimate conversion, but not one done by the source agency, and therefore not one designed to make constant dollar M1 or M2 an everyday economic statistic.

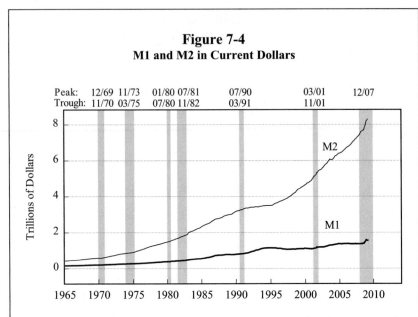

Figure 7-4
M1 and M2 in Current Dollars

Peak: 12/69 11/73   01/80 07/81   07/90   03/01   12/07
Trough: 11/70 03/75   07/80 11/82   03/91   11/01

The levels of M1 and M2 have leading indicator status only when converted to constant dollar amounts, a transformation not performed by the Federal Reserve System. When presented in seasonally adjusted current dollars, as in the figure here, they tell us very little about recessions and recoveries.

If anything, the sharp increase in both money measures in 2008-09 reflects the aggressive monetary policies of the Fed during that period. Finally, some studies have found a strong, if somewhat delayed, link between changes in the level of M2 and prices. Because of this, we also want to keep an eye on M2 since it may indicate changes in the inflation rate later on.

M1 and M2

Indicator status:	Both series: no value as indicators of recession or recovery
Compiled by:	Federal Reserve Board of Governors
Frequency:	Weekly
Release date:	4:30 p.m. Thursdays for the previous week
Revisions:	None
Published data:	*Statistical Release H.6,* Fed Board of Governors
	Federal Reserve Bulletin, Fed Board of Governors
Internet:	http://www.federalreserve.gov
	http://www.EconSources.com

Fed Funds Rate

Fed funds, or *federal funds,* are excess reserve balances that banks and other financial institutions lend to one another on a short-term basis. The interest paid to borrow these funds is known as the *fed funds rate*. Most loans are overnight, although some may be for as long as three days.

Fed Funds

Historically, member banks of the Federal Reserve System were required to keep deposits at the Fed as reserves against savings accounts and checking deposits. Since the Fed did not pay interest on these reserves, member banks had little incentive to keep more funds than they needed. However, if a bank had excess reserves, it would often lend the surplus to another member bank on an overnight or weekend basis for a small fee. Banks that borrowed the excess reserves often did so to shore up their own reserves at the Fed.

When the loans were made, the funds never really left the Fed—hence the term "federal" in the title. All a member bank needed to do to make a transaction was to notify the district Fed bank that reserve funds were to be transferred from its account to another bank's account for a short period of time, after which the funds would be transferred back. Today the market for fed funds is far more sophisticated and is dominated by brokers who facilitate transfers.[7]

Over time, federal funds took on a more generic meaning as the practice of borrowing one another's reserves expanded to financial institutions outside the Federal Reserve System.[8] Today, financial institutions tend to deal with one another through the Fed since all depository institutions have access.

---

[7] The daily effective fed funds rate is a weighted average of rates on trades through N.Y. brokers. Rates are annualized using a 360-day year.

[8] Nonmember state banks, for example, might lend reserves to one another under this system.

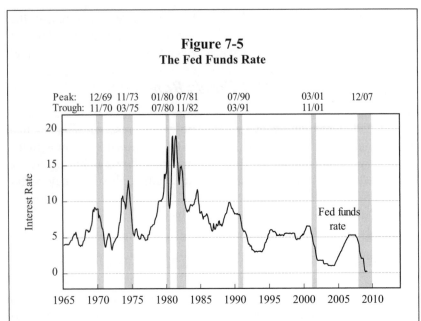

Figure 7-5
The Fed Funds Rate

Peak: 12/69 11/73   01/80 07/81   07/90   03/01   12/07
Trough: 11/70 03/75   07/80 11/82   03/91   11/01

Fed funds rate

Fed funds are short-term reserves that banks and other financial institutions lend to each other overnight, or for a few days at a time. The fed funds rate is the only interest rate that acts as a leading indicator for recessions.

A Leading Indicator

The history of the federal funds rate since 1965 is presented in Figure 7-5. Like many other interest rates in the economy, in recent years it has tended to act as a leading indicator for peaks in overall economic activity. This pattern is probably due to the Fed's increasingly proactive role in preventing or at least mitigating economic downturns. For example, if the economy shows signs of slowing or even entering a recession, the Fed may pump excess reserves into the banking system to add liquidity. This stimulates the economy by lowering the price that other banks pay for borrowed reserves.

The Fed is also likely to keep the rate relatively low until the recovery is well underway, so the fed funds rate does not begin to turn up until well after the recession has ended—making the series a lagging indicator for recoveries.

Actually, the phrase "relatively low" may misrepresent the situation somewhat as in early 2009 the fed funds rate was about as low as it could go. Economists were, of course, generally pleased that the Fed was working so aggressively to counter the recession—but once the rate effectively approaches or nearly reaches zero, there's not much else that the Fed can do.

Fed Funds Rate

Indicator status:	Leading for recessions; lagging for recoveries
Compiled by:	Federal Reserve Board of Governors
Frequency:	Daily
Release date:	Daily
Revisions:	None
Published data:	*Federal Reserve Bulletin*, Fed Board of Governors
	Statistical Release H.15, Fed Board of Governors
Internet:	http://www.federalreserve.gov
	http://www.EconSources.com

Primary Credit Rate

In its central bank role as a "lender of last resort," the Federal Reserve System is required to lend funds to other financial institutions, especially in times of need. Historically, the Fed used the *discount rate* to designate the interest rate on these borrowed funds. The term "discount rate" was, however, a misnomer since virtually all loans made by the Fed were in the form of advances rather than discounts. In addition, the discount rate was not even a competitive rate—it was instead a policy tool used to control the money supply.

In January 2003, the Fed introduced the *primary credit rate* as the successor to the discount rate. The main purpose of the new primary credit program was to make short-term credit available as a backup source of liquidity to generally sound institutions. Unchanged was the fact that Federal Reserve Banks would retain the discretion to not lend in circumstances that they thought were inconsistent with that purpose.

Early Development

When the Fed was first established in 1913, the discount rate was intended to be the primary tool of monetary policy. Soon, however, the Fed discovered it could also buy and sell government bonds to affect interest rates, a function now managed by the Federal Open Market Committee (FOMC).

It may seem redundant to have an independently determined discount rate coexist with FOMC activities, but this arrangement had two advantages for the Fed. First, the discount rate was set in conjunction with the regional Fed banks, fostering the appearance of participation in the monetary policy decision-making process.[9]

---

[9] An article in *Economic Commentary* by the Federal Reserve Bank of Cleveland explains how the discount rate is set:

> The mechanics of setting the discount rate are not complicated. The Board of Directors of each of the 12 Federal Reserve Banks is required to recommend a rate setting for its Bank to the Board of Governors of the Federal Reserve System no less frequently than every two weeks. If the Board of Governors approves the

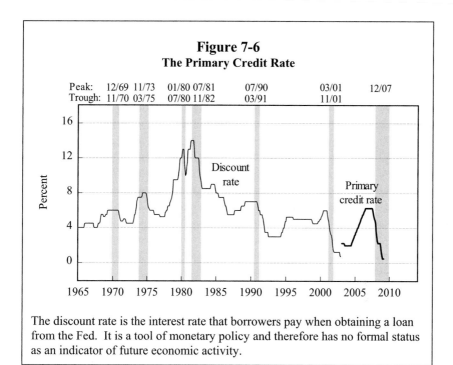

Figure 7-6
The Primary Credit Rate

Peak: 12/69 11/73 01/80 07/81 07/90 03/01 12/07
Trough: 11/70 03/75 07/80 11/82 03/91 11/01

The discount rate is the interest rate that borrowers pay when obtaining a loan from the Fed. It is a tool of monetary policy and therefore has no formal status as an indicator of future economic activity.

Second, it generated an "announcement effect" which served as a source of policy information for Fed watchers. The primary credit rate still serves many of these functions and is reflective of the evolutionary nature of the Fed.

Primary Credit Rate	
Indicator status:	None
Compiled by:	Federal Reserve Board of Governors
Frequency:	Daily
Release date:	Daily
Revisions:	None
Published data:	*Federal Reserve Bulletin,* Fed Board of Governors
	Statistical Release H.15, Fed Board of Governors
Internet:	http://www.federalreserve.gov
	http://www.EconSources.com

recommendation, typically it will notify any of the other 12 Banks that have not made the same recommendation so that their Boards of Directors have an opportunity to act simultaneously. If the Board of Governors thinks that a change is called for when none of the 12 Banks has recommended a change, it may make informal efforts to elicit a recommendation (July 15, 1989).

Treasury Bill Rate

The **Treasury bill rate** is one of the most important short-term interest rates in the economy. Treasury bills (T-bills) are available to a wide range of investors, and they are auctioned weekly and traded daily.[10] They are also popular with investors because they are among the safest of all possible investments. As a result, the rate on T-bills reflects the most current market forces of supply and demand.

The Historical Record

The history of interest rate movements for T-bills appears in Figure 7-7. For comparison purposes, the discount and the primary credit rates are also shown.

Since the T-bill rate adjusts so quickly to market forces, it behaves as a coincident indicator for peaks in the economy, meaning that the rate turns down when the economy turns down.

The T-bill Rate and the Fed

The T-bill rate also behaves as a lagging indicator when the economy recovers from a recession, meaning that the economy starts to grow again before the T-bill rate starts to rise. This is undoubtedly due to the Fed's efforts to keep interest rates low until it is sure that the economy has actually recovered. As a result, the series, like other interest rates, is a lagging indicator for recoveries.

Treasury bills are traded continuously during market hours, and so rates are available daily. Summary information is published by the Fed and most financial newspapers. Because the T-bill rate is so

---

[10] A Treasury bill is a short-term obligation with a maturity of 13, 26, or 52 weeks. T-bills have minimum denominations of $10,000 and do not pay interest directly because they are sold on a discount basis. For example, an investor may purchase a 52-week bill for $9,300. The $700 difference between the amount paid and the amount received at maturity is the investor's interest. The $700 return on the $9,300 investment is a yield of $700/$9,300 = 0.0753, or 7.53 percent.

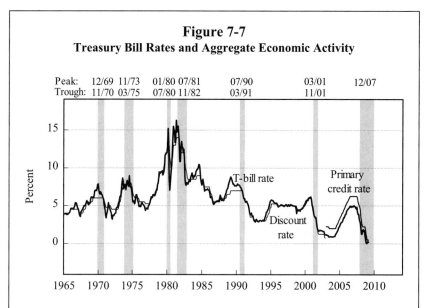

Figure 7-7
Treasury Bill Rates and Aggregate Economic Activity

| Peak: | 12/69 | 11/73 | 01/80 | 07/81 | 07/90 | 03/01 | 12/07 |
| Trough: | 11/70 | 03/75 | 07/80 | 11/82 | 03/91 | 11/01 |

The T-bill rate is one of the most competitive rates in the economy and a good indicator of changes in the supply and demand for funds. In comparison, the discount rate tends to be more of a lagging indicator.

competitive, many adjustable-rate financial securities, including some home mortgages, are tied to them.

Treasury Bill Rate

Indicator status:	Coincident for recessions; lagging for recoveries
Compiled by:	Federal Reserve Board of Governors
Frequency:	Daily
Release date:	Daily
Revisions:	None
Published data:	Most financial newspapers
	Economic Indicators, Council of Economic Advisors
	Federal Reserve Bulletin, Fed Board of Governors
	Statistical Release H.15, Fed Board of Governors
Internet:	http://www.federalreserve.gov
	http://www.EconSources.com

Prime Rate

Historically, the ***prime rate*** was the rate banks charged their best customers. Because of this, it received wide publicity as the lowest rate available from banks. Things have changed since then, and so the prime rate today is not quite the same as it used to be. Despite these changes, it is still widely watched.

If You Get the Prime Rate, Do You Actually Pay It?

That depends. Suppose a business borrows $100,000 at a 10 percent prime rate. However, the company may not get to use all the funds because the bank may require a *compensating balance*, or a deposit (usually interest free), in the amount of $5,000. On a simple interest basis, the company is really paying $10,000 for the use of $95,000, which computes to a 10.53 percent simple rate.

Another bank may have an identical prime but a different compensating balance requirement in the amount of $9,000 per $100,000 borrowed. A borrower at this bank would still pay 10 percent on the $100,000 for an interest cost of $10,000 but have access to only $91,000, for a 10.99 percent simple rate.

The Historical Record

The Fed determines the predominant prime rate by surveying the 25 largest banks in the country, shown in Table 7-3, as ranked by total asset size. Once the predominant prime is established, the Fed waits for the majority of the banks to adopt a new rate before the prime is recomputed.

Figure 7-8 shows that the prime rate appears to adjust in steps, or stages. That is, it stays at one level for a while before it adjusts to a new one. There are two reasons for this. First, banks are more inclined to change the compensating balance requirement than the prime, especially when interest rates are rising. Second, the official prime rate number compiled by the Fed represents the prevailing level

Table 7-3

Banks Used to Determine the Predominant Prime Rate

Boston	RBS Citizen's NA
	State Street Bank & Trust Company
New York	Goldman Sachs Bank USA
	Bank of New York Mellon
	Manufacturers & Traders TC
Philadelphia	TD Bank N.A.
Cleveland	JPMorgan Chase Bank
	US Bank N.A.
	National City Bank
	Keybank N.A.
	Fifth Third Bank
Richmond	Bank of America N.A.
	Wachovia Bank N.A.
	HSBC Bank USA N.A.
	Branch Bank & Trust Co.
	Capital One N.A.
Atlanta	SunTrust Bank
	Regions Bank
	Compass Bank
Chicago	Harris N.A.
Dallas	Comerica Bank
San Francisco	Citibank N.A.
	Union Bank N.A.
	Bank of the West
	Merrill Lynch Bank USA

Source: The Federal Reserve System, Division of Monetary Affairs, May 29, 3009.

—meaning the rate charged by the most banks in the sample—rather than an average of the existing rates charged by banks.

Because banks can increase effective interest rates by changing the compensating balance, the prime is a lagging indicator for both recessions and recoveries. Changes in the prime rate usually make headlines, but the changes normally reflect other interest rate adjustments that have already taken place. Occasionally, a prominent

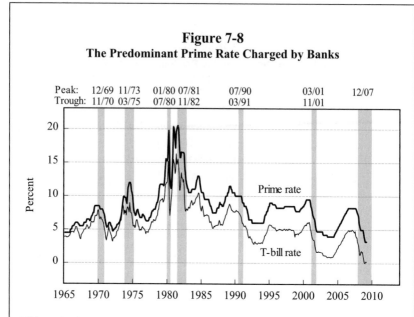

Figure 7-8
The Predominant Prime Rate Charged by Banks

Peak: 12/69 11/73   01/80 07/81   07/90   03/01   12/07
Trough: 11/70 03/75   07/80 11/82   03/91   11/01

This series is sometimes called the "average" prime rate charged by banks, but it's clearly *not* an average. If 13 banks in the Fed sample charge a prime rate of 7 percent, and if the remaining 12 charge 9 percent, the predominant prime will be 7 percent.

bank not on the list may change its rate, and the action may be widely reported in the press, but it will have no effect on the official predominant prime rate compiled by the Fed.

Prime Rate	
Indicator status:	Lagging for recessions and recoveries
Compiled by:	Federal Reserve Board of Governors
Frequency:	Daily
Release date:	Daily
Revisions:	None
Published data:	*Federal Reserve Bulletin*, Fed Board of Governors
	Statistical Release H.15, Fed Board of Governors
Internet:	http://www.federalreserve.gov
	http://www.EconSources.com

LIBOR

The **LIBOR**, or **London Interbank Offer Rate**, is the rate of interest that banks charge when they loan money to each other in the London wholesale money markets. The LIBOR rate is also the world's most widely used benchmark for short-term interest rates and, increasingly, US loans and even mortgages.

Why London?

Probably because London is arguably the world's largest and most important finance center. On top of that, the dollar is an international currency, so it's not surprising that a dollar-based interest rate measure was developed.

How is it Determined?

The LIBOR rate is fixed daily by the British Banker's Association (BBA).[11] Just before 11:00 a.m., the BBA conducts a survey of approximately 15 of the largest commercial banks in the London wholesale market. A handful of the banks are American banks, but the majority are non-US banks like the Bank of Tokyo-Mitsubishi (Japan), Deutsche Bank AG (Germany), the Royal Bank of Canada, and Barclays Bank (United Kingdom).

The BBA then asks each bank in the survey the rate they would have to pay if they were to borrow Eurodollars (dollar-denominated deposits in a bank outside the US) from other commercial banks. These data are collected for a range of maturities, and the rate is then published at about 11:30 a.m. This rate then remains unchanged until it is reestablished again the next day.

Because the banks are large competitive institutions, and because the Eurodollars that they lend each other are outside the control of the Federal Reserve System, the LIBOR rate is thought to be generally free of political and regulatory influence.

---

[11] The BBA is a nonprofit trade association.

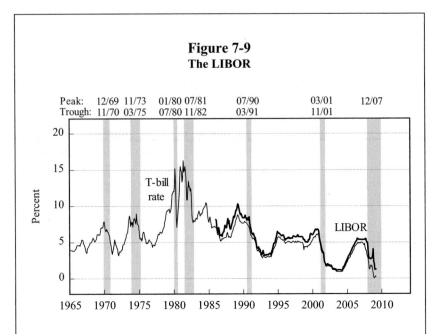

Figure 7-9
The LIBOR

The BBA's LIBOR reflects the actual rate at which large wholesale banks would borrow dollars from each other. It is established once a day based on a survey of about 15 large commercial banks.

The Historical Record

Figure 7-9 shows the American T-bill rate and BBA's LIBOR from its inception in January of 1986. The two rates follow each other fairly closely, although the LIBOR is the slightly higher of the two at any given time. In general, it is thought to be an accurate barometer of interest rates in a global market.

LIBOR	
Indicator status:	None, although it tracks the T-bill rate closely
Compiled by:	British Banker's Association
Frequency:	Daily at about 11:30 a.m. GMT
Revisions:	None
Published data:	Most financial newspapers

Chapter 8

STOCK PRICES and INTERNATIONAL TRADE

Dow Jones Industrial Average

The **Dow Jones Industrial Average** (**DJIA**) is one of the oldest and most widely-quoted measures of stock market performance in the world. It is used as a proxy for the price movements of stocks issued by more than 3,000 companies that are primarily listed on the New York Stock Exchange (NYSE).

The DJIA includes 30 representative firms, and the size of the index depends on the market price of each firm's stock at any given time. If the prices of the stocks in the average are rising, the DJIA goes up and the market is also presumed to be going up. If the prices of the 30 stocks are falling, the DJIA goes down, indicating that other stocks in the market are also presumed to be going down. Over time, some firms are deleted and others added, but the total number of stocks is kept at 30.

Early History

In 1884 the Dow Jones Corporation began to publish the average closing price of 11 active stocks in its *Customer's Afternoon Letter*, a short publication that later evolved into *The Wall Street Journal*. By 1886 the average included 12 stocks, and by 1916 it was expanded to 20.[1] Finally, in 1928 it was expanded to include 30 stocks. These stocks, listed in Table 8-1, have changed occasionally

---

[1] The Dow Jones Corporation has a complete history of the companies in the average dating from 1884 on its website at http://dowjones.com.

Table 8-1
The 30 Stocks in the Dow Jones Industrial Average

3M Company	Exxon Mobile	McDonald's
Alcoa Inc.	General Electric	Merck & Company
American Express	General Motors	Microsoft
AT&T	Hewlett-Packard	Pfizer Inc.
Bank of America	Intel Corporation	The Coca Cola Co.
Boeing Company	IBM	Procter & Gamble
Caterpillar Inc.	Home Depot	United Technologies
Chevron Corp.	Johnson & Johnson	Verizon Communications
Citigroup Inc.	J.P. Morgan Chase	Wal-Mart Stores
E. I. DuPont	Kraft Foods Inc.	Walt Disney Company

Source: *Dow Jones Corporation*, May 13, 2009

over the years to keep abreast of changes in the economy. Figure 8-1 shows one of the more popular charts used to present daily movements of the average.

But, Is It *Really* an Average?

In 1884 the index really was an average, but it proved difficult to maintain because of the problem caused by stock splits. For example, consider a simple DJIA which, on Monday, had three stocks priced $20, $30, and $40. The DJIA for that day would be ($20 + $30 + $40)/3 = $30, or simply 30. Next, suppose that nothing happens on Tuesday except for a two-for-one split of the $20 stock (instead of holding one share of a stock worth $20, someone now owns two shares worth $10, and so his or her wealth remains unchanged).

If we computed the DJIA on Tuesday by dividing the prices of three shares ($10, $30, and $40) by 3, the DJIA would drop to 26.7, even though investors would be no worse off than before. We could, however, compensate for the drop in the average by adjusting the *divisor*. Instead of dividing the sum of the prices by 3, we could divide by 2.667 so that the "average" would be ($10 + $30 + $40)/2.667 = 30, just as before.

Whenever a stock splits or whenever stocks on the list are replaced, the divisor can be adjusted to keep the overall average from being affected. Of course, this means that the divisor must be revised frequently. By 1939, for example, the divisor was about 15; by 1950 it was below 9, and by 1981 it had reached 1.3. On May 13, 2009, the divisor was 0.125661, which means that the DJIA computation was as follows:

$$DJIA = \frac{\text{sum of 30 prices}}{\text{divisor}} = \frac{\$1,063.32}{.125661} = 8,461.81$$

We can now definitely say that the Dow Jones Industrial Average really *is* an average . . . in a manner of speaking.

Are 30 Stocks Enough?

Despite the small number of stocks included in the DJIA, the companies are so large that the DJIA represents about 25 percent of the total value of all stocks on the New York Stock Exchange. As a result, the movement of the DJIA coincides fairly well with that of a large number of stocks on the exchange.[2]

The 30 companies in the DJIA do not represent the smaller companies on the exchange, nor do they normally represent other firms listed on the American Stock Exchange, or even any of the other regional exchanges around the country. In fact, until October 1999, all of the companies in the DJIA were listed exclusively on the NYSE. The exception occurred when Intel and Microsoft, companies listed on the NASDAQ, were added in an attempt to give a bigger role to technology stocks.

Why Update the DJIA?

The main reason for updating the companies in the DJIA is to make the sample more reflective of the changing conditions in the economy. For example, in April 1991, the composition of the index was changed to better reflect the size of the services sector. Navistar, Primerica, and USX were dropped from the index, while Caterpillar, Disney, and J.P. Morgan were added.

By the late 1990s, the NASDAQ was beginning to perform better than the DJIA—beating it three out of four years in a row. As a result, Intel and Microsoft took the place of Chevron and Goodyear even though they were listed on a different exchange. At the same

---

[2] For a long-term comparison, a chart of the DJIA appears with the S&P 500 in Figure 8-2 on page 141.

time, Union Carbide and Sears were dropped in place of SBC Communications and Home Depot. Subsequent to that, Altria Group, Eastman Kodak, Honeywell, International Paper, and SBC Communications were dropped in favor of Bank of America, Chevron, Kraft Foods, Pfizer, and Verizon Communications. This means that nearly half of the 30 firms in the sample were replaced in less than 15 years.

When firms are replaced in the DJIA, no historical revisions or other changes are made to the series. All that is done is to select a new divisor so that the DJIA remains unchanged during the transition. So, if a low-priced stock is replaced by a higher one, the divisor is increased on the following day.

Are There Other Things We Should Know?

There are two worth mentioning. First, any price-weighted average like the DJIA gives more weight to higher-priced stocks than it does to lower-priced ones. For example, a 10-percent increase of 3M stock (trading near $129 in July 2003) adds $12.90 to the numerator of the equation above. A 10-percent increase in the price of Alcoa (trading near $25 at the same time) adds only $2.50 to the numerator.

The other weakness of the DJIA is that it does not adjust for stock dividends of less than 10 percent.[3] This means that it understates long-term gains in the market. Stock prices will not tend to rise as fast if some companies declare relatively small and relatively frequent stock dividends.

Because the series is updated so frequently and because of the visibility given to it by the Dow Jones Corporation that publishes *The Wall Street Journal*, it is a useful measure of short-term movements of stock prices on (predominately) the New York Stock Exchange. When stock price movements over longer periods are of concern,

---

[3] Theoretically, a stock dividend (a dividend paid in stock, rather than cash) *lowers* the company's stock price. If a firm in the 30-company sample declares an 8 percent stock dividend, the number of shares outstanding goes up by 8 percent and the price goes down by a like amount—leaving investors with no change in net wealth. However, the divisor for the DJIA remains unchanged, so the DJIA would actually show a decline.

researchers usually turn to other series that have a broader sample and are not biased by stock dividend payouts.

Finally, the Dow Jones Industrial Average is regarded by many as a leading indicator of future economic activity, with the index turning down before a recession begins and then normally turning up before the economy turns up—although it did not turn up until well after the 2001 recession ended. It is not the series of stock prices used by The Conference Board for its *leading economic index* (Standard & Poor's 500 is used instead), but as you can see in Figure 8-2, the two series are fairly close.

Dow Jones Industrial Average

Indicator status:	Leading for peaks; *normally* leading for recoveries
Compiled by:	Dow Jones & Company
Frequency:	Almost continuously during market hours
Revisions:	None
Published data:	*The Wall Street Journal* and the stock market section of most newspapers
	Economic Indicators, Council of Economic Advisors
Internet:	http://dowjones.com
	http://www.EconSources.com

Standard & Poor's 500

Another popular measure of stock price performance is **Standard & Poor's 500** (**S&P 500**) composite index. Standard and Poor's Corporation published its first market index of 233 stocks in 1923. By 1957 the list had expanded to a total of 500 stocks. Today, those 500 stocks represent four major industry groupings: industrials, public utilities, transports, and finance.[4]

How Are the Firms in the Index Selected?

One criterion is based on industry groupings. The market is first divided into approximately 100 subgroups ranging from aerospace to toys. Then, representative companies are selected for each industry grouping. In some cases, the firms in the subgroups are relatively small, with modest stock issues outstanding. A second criterion is that the shares of a company are liquid enough to be fairly priced. Companies that are closely held, or do not otherwise have a competitive market for their shares, are excluded from the index.

Finally, and unlike the DJIA, the companies in the sub groupings are not primarily listed on the NYSE; many are listed on the American Stock Exchange and the NASDQ. While the S&P 500 companies do not necessarily include the largest ones on the New York Stock Exchange, approximately 80 percent of the total value of all NYSE stocks is represented in the index.

How Is the Index Computed?

The S&P 500 is not a price-weighted average like the DJIA; it is a *market value-weighted index* reflecting the total market value of a company's stock. For each company in the sample, the total number

---

[4] Until 1988, the 500 stocks consisted of 400 industrials, 40 utilities, 20 transportation companies, and 40 financial institutions. When a company in one category was dropped, it was replaced by another company from the same category. The number of companies in each category now varies somewhat over time.

of shares outstanding is multiplied by the individual price per share to get the total market value of that stock.[5] The market value for each of the remaining 499 stocks is computed in the same way, and the results are added together to get the current market value of all 500 stocks in the index. The resulting total would be huge, but when indexed to a 1941-1943 base period, the numbers are more manageable.

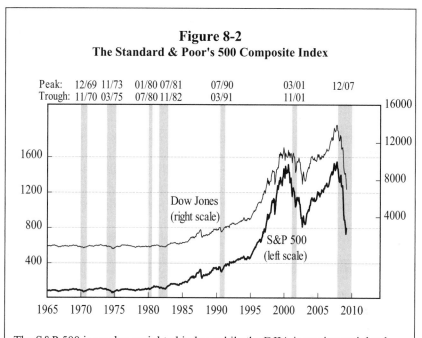

Figure 8-2
The Standard & Poor's 500 Composite Index

The S&P 500 is a value-weighted index, while the DJIA is a price-weighted index. Despite this difference and the difference in sample size, the two series behave in a similar manner over time.

The S&P 500 series in Figure 8-2 is different from most other indices in that it has a base value of 10 rather than 100. So, if the index closes at 1250, the total market value of all stocks in the S&P 500 is 125 times higher (1250/10) than it was in the 1941-1943 period.

---

[5] To illustrate, a company with 3 million shares of common stock outstanding, valued at $15 a share, would have a total market value of (3,000,000)($15) = $45,000,000.

Is the S&P 500 Better Than the DJIA?

Different perhaps, but not necessarily better. It is more representative since 500 stocks are covered rather than 30. In addition, the value-weighted nature of the index means that it automatically adjusts for splits and stock dividends.[6] As can be seen in Figure 8-2, the S&P 500 and the DJIA are fairly close despite the difference in the sample size used by each.

In addition to its role as a proxy for stock price movements, the index generally works so well as a leading indicator of future economic activity that it is used in The Conference Board's *of leading economic index.*

```
┌──────────────────────── Standard & Poor's 500 ────────────────────────┐
```

Indicator status:	Leading for recessions and recoveries
Compiled by:	Standard & Poor's Corporation
Frequency:	Almost continuously
Release date:	Daily
Revisions:	None
Published data:	Stock report listing in most daily papers
	Economic Indicators, Council of Economic Advisors
Internet:	http://www.standardandpoors.com
	http://www.EconSources.com

---

[6] Suppose that a company listed in the S&P 500 declares a 5 percent stock dividend. The number of shares would go up by 5 percent and the price of the shares would go down by a corresponding amount, leaving the total market value of the stock—and the level of the S&P 500—unchanged. If that same company happened to be one of the 30 DJIA stocks, the index would fall slightly because the price of one of the stocks in the numerator would fall, *without* any compensating change in the divisor.

Russell 3000

Another useful measure of stock market performance is the *Russell 3000* index. Because it includes 3,000 stocks, and because the index represents approximately 98 percent of all U.S. equity market capital, it is even more comprehensive than the S&P 500. However, and unlike most of our other economic statistics, the Russell 3000 is produced by a private, for-profit company to evaluate the performance of other for-profit companies.

Specifically, the index is designed to gauge the performance of stock fund managers who normally refer to their portfolios in terms of the value of the "assets"—the number of shares times their price— they manage. Since most portfolio managers manage thousands or even millions of shares in hundreds of companies, portfolios asset values can be huge. For this reason the Russell 3000 is a popular performance measure for stock and mutual fund managers.

How is the Index Constructed?

First, only companies incorporated in the United States and its territories are eligible for inclusion. Next, all U.S. common stocks are ranked from largest to smallest according to market capitalization (number of shares outstanding times market share price). The largest 3,000 companies are then used for the Russell 3000 index.[7]

The total market capitalization of 3,000 stocks would be huge, of course, so the series was indexed to a base of 100 for December 1978, the initial month of the series. So, if the index should close today at a value of 580, then the total market capitalization of the largest 3,000 stocks would be exactly 5.8 times higher (580/100 = 5.8) than it was in December of 1978. Day-to-day changes, or year-to-date changes, are generally reported in terms of absolute as well as percentage changes.

---

[7] There are some other exceptions: stocks trading for less than $1 a share are excluded from the survey, as are bulletin board and pink sheet stocks, limited partnerships, royalty trusts, and ADRs.

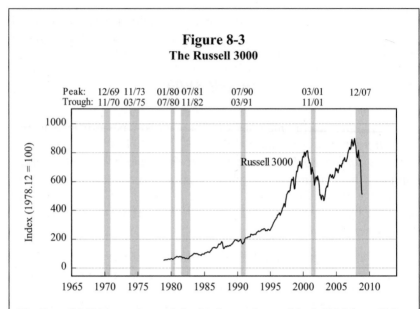

Figure 8-3
The Russell 3000

| Peak: | 12/69 | 11/73 | 01/80 | 07/81 | 07/90 | 03/01 | 12/07 |
| Trough: | 11/70 | 03/75 | 07/80 | 11/82 | 03/91 | 11/01 | |

The Russell 3000 is a value-weighted index made up of the 3,000 largest U.S. companies based on market capitalization. Like most other stock indices, it behaves more as a leading indicator for both recessions and recoveries.

The Russell 3000 is also divided into two other indices. The 1,000 firms with the largest capitalization make up the Russell 1000, or "large cap" index. The next 2,000 firms make up the Russell 2000, or "small cap" index. The three Russell indices are like the S&P 500 in that they are market value-weighted indices. Unlike the S&P, however, no value judgments are made with respect to selecting representative firms as inclusion is based entirely on market capitalization.

How Often Is the Index Updated?

Over time, a firm's market capitalization changes whenever the price of its stock changes, or whenever the number of outstanding shares changes. In addition, there are always some mergers and bankruptcies which could affect the capitalization of the 3,000 companies in the series. Because of this, the index has to be reconstituted on a regular basis.

At first, from 1979 to 1986, the indices were rebalanced quarterly. Then, from 1987 until 1989, they were reconstituted semiannually. Since then, the indices were adjusted annually as of market capitalizations on May 31st. As for justifying the now annual adjustments, Russell claims that so many mutual funds offer investments tied to the Russell indices that more frequent revisions would require the funds to "buy and sell stocks each time the index is reconstituted to ensure that they continue to mimic the index ... [thereby inflicting] high transaction costs on index funds."[8]

The Historical Record

As for its value as a predictive economic indicator, the performance of the Russell 3000 is shown in Figure 8-3. At times the series exhibits characteristics of a leading indicator, going down before a recession begins and then recovering before the expansion starts. At other times, as following the 2001 recession, it behaves in more of a lagging manner. Even though the series only dates back to 1978, it would help to have a few more economic expansions and recessions for comparison before we make a definitive judgment.

Russell 3000	
Indicator status:	Leading for recessions
Compiled by:	Frank Russell Company, 590 Madison Avenue, New York, NY 10022
Frequency:	Daily
Release date:	Daily
Revisions:	Annually on May 31st
Published data:	Stock report listing in most daily papers
Internet:	http://www.russell.com
	http://www.EconSources.com

---

[8] *Q&A Examining the Construction and Purpose of the Russell Indices*, www.russell.com, July 12, 2003.

Wilshire 5000

The broadest measure of overall stock market performance is provided by the *Wilshire 5000 Total Market Index*. The index is designed as a comprehensive market measure that covers all of the stocks traded in the major U.S. equity markets. Like other stock market indices, the Wilshire 5000 is produced by a for-profit company, and the index is often used as a benchmark to compare the performance of stock and mutual fund managers in other for-profit companies.

How is the Index Constructed?

When the index was first created in 1974, there were approximately 5,000 companies in the index. Since then, the number of companies in the index changed with the number of firms listed on the NYSE, AMEX, and NASDAQ—with the total listing approximating, but never equaling, 5,000.[9] Each of these companies must be headquartered, and their stock issues must also be traded, in the U.S. to be eligible for the index. If a company has more than one class of stock, then the various stock issues are combined into a primary issue for purposes of computing total market capitalization (number of shares times market value). Finally, the index is reconstituted monthly to account for firms that have entered the market, merged, or gone bankrupt.

The market capitalization of the index was $1,404.6 billion on December 31, 1980—this is also the base value for the index. So, if the index closed at 8,999.4 on May 13, 2009 (which was its actual closing value), then the market increased by a factor of 6.4 (or 8,999.4/1,404.6 = 6.4) over the same period. The published index number we see for the Wilshire 5000, then, is the total market capitalization of all U.S. stocks at that time.

---

[9] Visit http://www.wilshire.com/Indexes/Broad/Wilshire5000/Characteristics.html to get the total number of companies—those on the NYSE, AMEX, and NASDAQ—that make up the Wilshire 5000 index.

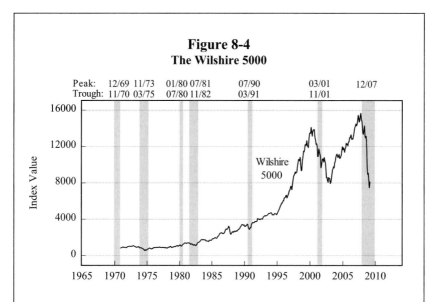

Figure 8-4
The Wilshire 5000

The Wilshire 5000 is a value-weighted index based on the market capitalization of approximately 5,000 companies. This index, like other stock indices, tends to behave as a leading indicator for both recessions.

The Historical Record

Most stock market indices behave as leading indicators for both recessions and recoveries. The Wilshire 5000 is no different, although it clearly was slow to recover after the recession of 2001. How it behaves with respect to the recovery that follows the 2008-09 recession is yet to be seen, but we should realize that none of our forecasting tools are perfect—which is why we look at more than one at any given time.

Wilshire 5000	
Indicator status:	Leading for recessions
Compiled by:	Wilshire Associates, Inc, New York, NY 10022
Frequency:	Daily
Release date:	Daily
Revisions:	None
Published data:	Stock report listing in most daily papers
Internet:	http://www.wilshire.com
	http://www.EconSources.com

Trade Deficit

When a country engages in international trade, several formal sets of accounts are used to track the flow of international transactions. The best known is the *balance on goods and services* that replaced the *balance on merchandise trade* account in 1994.[10] The word "balance" in the title allows for the possibility of a surplus as well as a deficit. However, because imports have exceeded exports for so long, our international trade statistics are commonly—although improperly—called the *deficit on goods and services* accounts.

NIPA (Again)

Trade statistics, like many other statistics generated by the U.S. Department of Commerce, are directly related to the national income and product accounts. Table 8-2 (a version of Table 2-3 on page 29) follows the familiar approach of dividing the economy into sectors. This time we want to focus on the foreign sector, otherwise known as "net exports of goods and services," to see how the *balance on goods and services* is computed.

The advanced first-quarter estimate in current dollars for 2009 show the total value of all exports at $1,536.7 billion. This was offset by imports of $1,874.4 billion, leaving a $337.7 billion deficit in the balance on goods and services. These numbers are reported on an annualized basis and show the net balance that would occur if exports and imports remained unchanged at the current rate for the entire year. The export and import categories are further divided into goods (merchandise) and services, with the table showing goods exports of $994.5 billion and imports of $1,491.0 billion—from which we can calculate (but do not show) a $496.5 billion deficit on goods alone.[11]

---

[10] At the time, the services component of the trade balance was running a substantial surplus, so the overall impact of combining goods with services was to sharply reduce the trade deficit.

[11] This is the *balance on merchandise trade* which has been in deficit continuously since the first quarter of 1976.

Table 8-2

NIPA and the Goods and Services Trade Balance, Billions of Dollars

	Current	Constant (2000$)	%GDP
Gross domestic product	*$14,075.5*	*$11,340.9*	*100.0*
Personal consumption expenditures	*9,955.7*	*8,214.2*	*70.7*
Gross private domestic investment	*1,579.8*	*1,329.8*	*11.2*
Net exports of goods and services	*-337.7*	*-308.4*	*-2.4*
Exports	*1,536.7*	*1,331.0*	*10.9*
Goods	994.5	882.7	7.1
Services	542.2	444.8	3.6
Imports	*1,874.4*	*1,639.5*	*13.3*
Goods	1,491.0	1,347.0	10.6
Services	383.4	288.6	2.7
Government consumption & gross investment	*2,877.7*	*2,073.8*	*20.4*

Source: *Bureau of Economic Analysis*. First quarter 2009 advance estimates; some totals may not add due to rounding.

Collecting and Reporting the Data

In practice, data for exports and imports of goods are collected continuously by the Census Bureau from declarations filed with the U.S. Customs Office by international shippers. Other techniques are used to estimate the monthly volume of services. Because of the nature of the data, trade figures are normally released 45 days after the close of the reference month.

The Census Bureau releases trade figures in several formats. Initial trade figures are reported monthly, and year-to-date figures are obtained by adding up the trade balances for individual months. Annualized figures, such as those shown in Table 8-2 and Figure 8-5, are estimated by the BEA and published as part of the NIPA. This means that the size of the trade deficit will be small if the report is for the month, approximately 3 times larger if the report is for the quarter, and approximately 12 times larger if the numbers are annualized. Accordingly, we have to be careful not to confuse a relatively large monthly figure with a relatively small quarterly one.

In Figure 8-5, annualized quarterly data are used to show the balance on goods and services from 1958 to the present. The balance can either be shown as the difference between overall goods and services exports and overall imports (shown at the top of the graph), or it can be plotted separately as shown at the bottom of the figure.

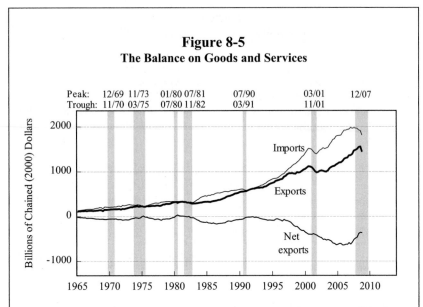

Figure 8-5
The Balance on Goods and Services

The United States has had a persistent goods (merchandise trade) deficit since the first quarter of 1976. The balance on goods and services, shown as the difference between the two series at the top, or plotted separately in the lower part of the figure, provides a more comprehensive measure of the trade picture.

Finally, we still don't have the whole international picture unless we take a look at the *balance on current account* which requires two further adjustments to the net exports of goods and services. First, we have to add income generated from U.S. assets held abroad, and then subtract any payments made because of foreign assets in the U.S. Second, we have to take into account net unilateral transfers made abroad: government grants to other nations; pension and social security payments to people living in other countries; and, payments made by private individuals to family members, political organizations, and religious movements in other countries.[12]

Despite the more comprehensive measure provided by the current account balance, the trade balance on goods and services shown in Figure 8-5 is perhaps our primary international trade statistic, or at least the one that gets the most attention. This series, in

---

[12] It also takes more time to get an accurate balance on the current account figures because of the time it takes to get these additional numbers.

turn, is affected by (1) our demand for foreign-made products and (2) our ability to sell domestically produced goods abroad. The trade figures on goods and services are important because they affect employment in the export and import industries as well as the value of the U.S. dollar.[13] Because dollars are paid to foreigners to make up for the deficit, larger deficits generally mean that more dollars go abroad, and more dollars circulating relative to other currencies make the dollar worth less.

Balance on Goods and Services

Indicator status:	None
Compiled by:	Census Bureau
Frequency:	Monthly, quarterly
Release date:	45 days after close of reporting month
Revisions:	One month back for seasonally adjusted data; 6 months back for constant dollar series; annual revisions in June
Published data:	*Report FT900*, Census Bureau
	Economic Indicators, Council of Economic Advisors
Internet:	http://www.census.gov/foreign-trade/www
	http://www.EconSources.com

---

[13] The relationship between the value of the dollar and the trade deficit is fairly straightforward. A strong dollar, as was the case in the mid-1980s, usually causes imports to rise faster than exports, which causes the trade balance to worsen. Eventually, the additional dollars that go abroad cause the international value of the dollar to fall, which reverses the trend in exports and imports and improves the trade balance.

International Value of the Dollar

When we talk about the value of the dollar, we are referring to its purchasing power in terms of other currencies. However, we can't evaluate the strength of the dollar by following just one or two exchange rates. Instead, we have to see how the dollar performs against a broader group or bundle of currencies. Historically, the key measure was called the *exchange*, or *trade-weighted value of the U.S. dollar,* and the Federal Reserve System prepared it.

Over time, however, world trade patterns changed and currency evolutions such as the emergence of the European Union's euro took place. As a result, the Fed retired the old series and replaced it with a broader one called the *broad currency index*. This new series has two components, one of which overlaps the old series.

Out With the Old . . .

The original series was created when the world went to flexible exchange rates in 1971. At the time, the Fed decided to compile an index using a group of 10, or G-10, major industrialized countries that were substantially involved in world trade.[14] The weight of each country's currency was based on the amount of global trade each one had relative to the other countries in 1971, the year flexible exchange rates were adopted. After the relative weights were determined, the series was given a base of 100 for March 1973.

During this period, the G-10 index, illustrated in Figure 8-6, served as the main measure of the dollar's strength.[15] The series went up when the dollar got stronger, and went down when the dollar got weaker relative to the other 10 currencies.

---

[14] The ten countries in the sample—Belgium, Canada, France, Germany, Italy, Japan, Netherlands, Sweden, Switzerland and the United Kingdom—were also chosen because they participated in the Smithsonian Accord of December 1971.

[15] The term "G-10" did not seem to come into use until after the Fed introduced the new broad currency index. As a result, the term "exchange" or "trade-weighted value of the dollar" is still applied to the new series by some parts of the Fed.

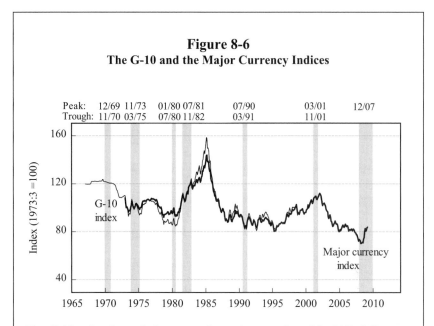

Figure 8-6
The G-10 and the Major Currency Indices

Peak:	12/69 11/73	01/80 07/81	07/90	03/01	12/07
Trough:	11/70 03/75	07/80 11/82	03/91	11/01	

The *G-10 index*, formerly known as the *exchange value of the U.S. dollar*, was our most comprehensive measure of the dollar's international strength until it was discontinued in 1998. The *major currency index* that takes its place is a subset of the new *broad currency index*.

Eventually the 1971 fixed base weights became outdated, and the introduction of the euro affected five of the ten currencies in the index. As a result, the G-10 index was discontinued in 1998.

. . . And In With the New

The more comprehensive replacement series is simply called the ***broad currency index***, and is made up of currencies from 35 countries. Unlike the G-10 index, the weights are not fixed, but are adjusted over time as trade patterns change. This index is computed in both nominal and real (inflation adjusted) terms, but the latter is the one most important for historical comparisons.

On a nominal or current dollar basis, the broad index started with a value of 32 in 1973, and then it increases steadily after that. While this may seem odd, the broad index contained a number of high-inflation countries that experienced severe currency

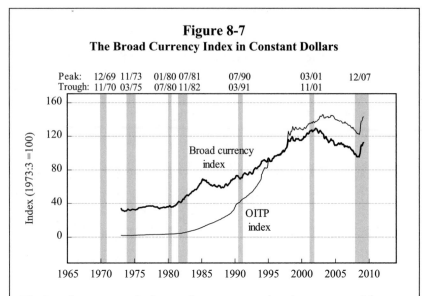

Figure 8-7
The Broad Currency Index in Constant Dollars

The *broad currency index* is now the most comprehensive measure of the International value of the dollar. The series includes both the *major currency index* and the *Other Important Trading Partner (OITP) index.*

depreciations, which helped drive up the demand for the dollar. When the series is converted to real terms, as in Figure 8-7, the basic trend of the U.S. dollar's value is more apparent, with the dollar being relatively strong in March 1985, and then getting much stronger after that.

A subset of the broad index is the ***major currency index***. This series has 16 countries and is more comparable to the G-10 index, which is why the two are shown together in Figure 8-6. Even though the weighting and sample sizes are different, it is clear that the two series behave about the same.

The last series is the ***OITP index***, which is short for "other important trading partners." This index consists of 19 countries that are in the broad index, but excludes those in the major currency index.[16] Many of the currencies of these countries are not traded

---

[16] The OITP includes currencies from Argentina, Brazil, Chile, China, Columbia, Hong Kong, Israel, India, Indonesia, Korea, Malaysia, Mexico, Russia, Saudi Arabia, Singapore, Taiwan, Thailand, the Philippines, and, Venezuela.

extensively outside their home markets, although they are important U.S. trading partners. Because many of these countries also experienced high inflation and occasional currency problems, the OITP index is computed in price-adjusted, or real terms, whenever long periods of time are involved. For shorter periods, any of the series in nominal terms are adequate.

So Why Are These Series Important?

The large changes in the international value of the dollar shown in Figures 8-6 and 8-7 have an enormous impact on the nation's exports and imports—and hence employment in those industries. When the purchasing power of the dollar is high, as in the mid-1980s, a large number of products are imported, leading to employment growth in those industries that utilize these imports. At the same time, however, American products are much more expensive abroad, leading to layoffs in the export industries. These forces are reversed when the value of the dollar falls, as it did in the early 1990s, causing a feast or famine situation for everyone as the dollar goes from strength to weakness, and then eventually back to strength again.

All of these forces also show up in the overall balance of trade. When the purchasing power of the dollar is high, imports are relatively inexpensive and our exports relatively costly to foreign buyers, which eventually results in a worsening balance of trade. When the value of the dollar falls, the situation tends to reverse itself, resulting in an improved balance of trade.

Value of the U.S. Dollar	
Indicator status:	None
Compiled by:	Federal Reserve Board of Governors
Frequency:	*H.10* weekly; *G.5* monthly
Release date:	*H.10* Monday for the previous week ending Friday,;
	G.5 last day of month for the reporting month
Revisions:	None
Published data:	*Federal Reserve Bulletin,* Fed Board of Governors
	Statistical Release G.5, for monthly rates
	Statistical Release H.10, for daily rates
Internet:	http://www.federalreserve.gov
	http://www.EconSources.com

Foreign Exchange

When we talk about foreign exchange in the context of international trade or finance, we are usually referring to the number of other currency units that can be purchased with one U.S. dollar. The amount of foreign currency that can be purchased with the dollar is called the *foreign exchange rate*, and there are well over 200 exchange rates in the world today.

Currency Units per Dollar and Dollar Equivalents

One popular way to express an exchange rate is in *American terms*, or in the number of U.S. dollars needed to buy a single foreign currency unit. For example, if one euro costs $1.3558, then 1.3558 is the U.S. dollar equivalent of one euro. Likewise, if the cost of a single yen is $0.01047, the U.S. dollar equivalent of one yen is 0.01047.

Table 8-3
Selected Foreign Exchange Rates

	U.S. $ Equivalents (American terms)	Foreign Currency Units per U.S. $ (European terms)
Japan (Yen)	0.01047	95.530
Mexico (peso)	0.07478	13.372
Switzerland (SFranc)	0.90106	1.1098
U.K. (Pound)	1.51160	0.66155
E.U. (Euro)	1.35580	0.73757

Source: *Wall Street Journal,* data are for May 13, 2009.

The second way to express an exchange rate is in *European terms*, or in the number of foreign currency units that are equal to one U.S. dollar. The two terms are simply reciprocals and are shown in Table 8-3 above. For example, if one euro costs $1.3558, then one dollar is worth 0.73757 Euros (0.73757 is the reciprocal of 1.3558).

Likewise, one dollar would be equal to 95.530 yen (the reciprocal of 1.01047).

Currency Cross Rates

If we want to know the exchange rate between two currencies, we could express everything in terms of cross rates, as in Table 8-4. This is especially helpful when neither of the currencies being traded is the U.S. dollar.

Table 8-4
Currency Cross Rates

	U.S. $	Euro	Pound	SFranc	Peso	Yen
Japan	95.530	129.52	144.40	86.079	7.1439	–.–
Mexico	13.372	18.130	20.214	12.049	–.–	0.13998
Switzerland	1.1098	1.5047	1.6776	–.–	0.08299	0.01162
U.K.	0.66155	0.89693	–.–	0.59610	0.04947	0.00693
Euro	0.73757	–.–	1.1149	0.66460	0.05516	0.00772
U.S.	–.–	1.3558	1.5116	0.90106	0.07478	0.01047

Source: Computed from Table 8-3 (reciprocals may not match due to rounding)

In the table, the value of each currency unit is expressed in terms of other currencies. For example, if one U.S. dollar buys 1.1098 SFrancs, and if one U.S. dollar buys 13.372 Mexican pesos, then one SFranc is worth 13.372/1.1098 = 12.049 Mexican pesos. Likewise, if a dollar can purchase 95.530 yen, and if a dollar can purchase 0.73757 euros, then one euro is worth 129.57 Japanese yen.

Foreign Exchange Rates	
Indicator status:	None
Compiled by:	Federal Reserve Board of Governors
Frequency:	*Statistical Releases G.5* monthly; *H.10* weekly; daily
Release date:	*H.10* Monday for the previous week ending Friday; *G.5* last day of month for the reporting month
Revisions:	None
Published data:	*The Wall Street Journal* for previous the day *Statistical Release H.10*, for daily NYC noon buying rates
Internet:	http://www.federalreserve.gov http://www.EconSources.com

Appendix

Chain Weighting

Chain-weighted calculations are hardly intuitive, so they are probably best explained with an example such as the one below which has only two product groups: computers and everything else. Before we begin, we should note that the examples are loosely modeled after Table 2-1 on page 17 of the text. You may want to review that table first before proceeding.

In the first year of our abbreviated economy, 2 units (Q) of computers are sold at an average price (P) of $10. Five units of everything else are sold at $10, generating a first-year GDP of $70. Similar calculations for the next year show a new GDP of $99, a 41.43 percent gain over the first. In tabular form, the data would look like this:

Table 1
GDP Growth in Current Dollars

Year 1	Q	P	(P)(Q)	Year 2	Q	P	(P)(Q)
Computers:	2	$10	$20	Computers:	4	$6	$24
Everything Else:	5	10	50	Everything Else:	5	15	75
			GDP = $70				GDP = $99

One-year growth in GDP = $99/$70 = 1.4143, or 41.43%

And yet, a closer look at Year 2 reveals that the robust 41.43 percent growth was due almost entirely to inflation in the "everything else" category. In fact, because computer prices went down so much, consumers only spent $4 more on computers in year 2 than they did in the previous year.

If we try to compensate for inflation by using base-year prices that are fixed in the first year, as in Table 2, we can see that the estimated growth for GDP is quite different, and much lower:

Table 2
GDP Growth Using Constant (Year 1) Prices

Year 1				Year 2			
	Q	P	(P)(Q)		Q	P	(P)(Q)
Computers:	2	$10	$20	Computers:	4	$10	$40
Everything Else:	5	10	50	Everything Else:	5	10	50
		GDP =	$70			GDP =	$90

One-year growth in GDP = $90/$70 = 1.2857, or 28.57%

Or, we could compute GDP growth using constant year 2 prices as in Table 3, which gives us an even *lower* growth estimate:

Table 3
GDP Growth Using Constant (Year 2) Prices

Year 1				Year 2			
	Q	P	(P)(Q)		Q	P	(P)(Q)
Computers:	2	$6	$12	Computers:	4	$6	$24
Everything Else:	5	15	75	Everything Else:	5	15	75
		GDP =	$87			GDP =	$99

One-year growth in GDP = $99/$87 = 1.1379, or 13.79%

If we want to adjust for inflation by using a set of fixed or base year prices, which of the two methods is theoretically superior: estimates using first year prices, or estimates using second year prices? Both have advantages and disadvantages, but it is clear that there is a "weighting effect"—a distortion that takes place because those quantities which have increased the most are usually associated with goods, such as computers, whose prices have declined the most relative to other prices.

The solution to the problem of the optimal base year is to find the geometric mean of the two index numbers. This is done by computed the square root of their product. In other words, the computations would appear as:

$$\sqrt{(1.2857)(1.1379)} = 1.2095, \text{ or } 20.95\%$$

This geometric average is also called the "Fisher Ideal" index number, and is the basis for BEA's chain-weighted prices that are now used in place of the fixed base-year weighted prices employed until 1995.

Despite the theoretical superiority of the geometric mean, BEA's changeover at the beginning of 1996 was not without controversy. For example, second quarter growth in 1995, formerly reported at +0.5 percent, was revised downward by 0.7 percent to -0.2 percent. Likewise, the revisions also meant that the growth of real GDP during recent expansions was actually 0.5 percent less than previously reported.

Index